D0744075

INTENSIVE ORCHARDING

managing your high production apple planting

TECHNICAL EDITOR
A. Brooke Peterson

Published by GOOD FRUIT GROWER, Yakima, Washington

Copyright ©1989
by Washington State Fruit Commission
All rights reserved

Published by:
Good Fruit Grower, a division of
Washington State Fruit Commission
1005 Tieton Drive, Yakima, WA 98902
509/575-2315 (telephone)
509/453-4880 (fax)

First printing 1989
Second printing February 1992

Printed and bound in the United States of America

ISBN 0-9630659-2-0

AUTHORS

Tom Auvil: Horticulturist, Grower, Trout, Inc., Chelan, Washington

Bruce H. Barritt: Professor of Horticulture, Tree Fruit Research and Extension Center, Washington State University, Wenatchee, Washington

Jim Fleming: Orchard Manager, Auvil Fruit Company, Vantage, Washington

H. George Geldart: Agricultural Economist, British Columbia Ministry of Agriculture and Fisheries, Vernon, British Columbia, Canada

Garth Kunz: Grower, Osyoos, British Columbia, Canada

A. Brooke Peterson: Tree Fruit Extension Agent, Washington State University, Yakima, Washington

Curt R. Rom: Formerly Assistant Professor/Horticulturist, Department of Horticulture and Landscape Architecture, Washington State University, Pullman, Washington

Paul Tvergyak: Tree Fruit Extension Agent, Washington State University, Wenatchee, Washington

K. Bert van Dalfsen: Agricultural Engineer, British Columbia Ministry of Agriculture and Fisheries, Abbotsford, British Columbia, Canada

Kathleen M. Williams: Extension Horticulturist, Tree Fruit Research and Extension Center, Washington State University, Wenatchee, Washington

TABLE OF

CONTENTS

INTRODUCTION

By A. Brooke Peterson

THE APPLE INDUSTRY IN NORTH AMERICA HAS PROGRESSED TOWARD higher density plantings from the start.

Early commercial orchards contained trees planted 40 by 40 feet apart. Over several decades, trees were planted ever closer together. Common tree spacings evolved to 20 by 20 feet to 10 by 20 feet, or 12 by 18 feet.

This change in orchard design (or, more accurately, to smaller trees) was partly due to a change in varieties. During this time span, Delicious became the main variety planted.

Currently, there are three principal factors forcing increased orchard intensification, all economic in nature. Whether the money for a new orchard comes out of the grower's pocket or is borrowed, the interest cost on the money invested is now being recognized as one of the major costs in establishing a new orchard. In order to reduce this interest expense, or lost income opportunity if the invested money is the grower's own, the orchard must begin bearing quickly.

Labor cost, one of the major expenses in orcharding, is

reduced with smaller trees. This is the second reason for planting more intensively.

The third factor is that high density orchards can be renewed more frequently. With rapidly changing consumer preferences for different varieties, it is imperative to have the flexibility to convert orchards to the more marketable varieties. This is difficult with low density orchards that are slow coming into production.

Along with the increased intensification of orchard plantings, comes increased intensification of orchard management. Different, more precocious, size-controlling rootstocks must be used. Tree support is not an option, it is a requirement. The ability to understand tree growth, how trees respond to pruning and training, the necessity of tree support and control of vegetative growth, all take on added emphasis.

These concerns are behind this book on high density tree management. It is the intention of the authors to provide practical, yet detailed information on how trees are best managed under high density.

1 BASIC CONCEPTS IN PRUNING AND TRAINING

By A. Brooke Peterson

THE SUCCESSFUL MANAGEMENT OF APPLE TREES UNDER ANY PRUNING and training system depends on understanding a few simple concepts. It does not matter whether the orchard is low density or high density, trellised or freestanding.

The same important concepts must be understood and properly applied for optimum tree performance. Higher density orchards move more rapidly into a mature, producing condition, and there is physically less space between trees. Therefore, errors in tree management or a failure to understand the important principles in pruning and training are potentially more serious.

The important basic concepts in pruning and training can be listed as follows:

1) Fruiting habit;
2) Growth habit;
3) Apical dominance; and
4) Type of pruning cuts.

Why prune and train apple trees?

It has long been a horticultural practice to prune newly planted trees to restore the balance between root and shoot growth. In a higher density orchard system, pruning of newly planted trees is generally minimized, because fruiting is delayed. This implies that earlier planting into properly prepared soil is more important under increased tree densities, so that sufficient springtime root growth can occur before increased demands are placed on the root system.

In young trees, pruning and training is done so that the trees will develop a strong framework of fruiting branches that are easily accessible for fruit thinning and picking, chemical applications, and light interception. As the tree matures, pruning is continued to remove excessive growth and limit tree size. Finally, pruning and training is used to recycle and stimulate production of young, strong fruiting wood for improved fruit quality and size.

The fruiting habit

In every species of fruit, the development of blossom buds, flowers, and fruit occurs in a manner which is characteristic of that species.

In apple, as well as pear, mixed buds which have flowers and spur leaves characteristically develop as the terminal bud of a shoot. Lateral buds located along the previous season's shoot growth are generally leaf or vegetative buds. From these buds develop either long shoots or shorter shoots called "spurs." The shorter shoots or spurs often terminate with a blossom bud.

This pattern or rhythm of growth results in the typical terminal vegetative growth the first year, the development of lateral shoots or spurs with blossom buds the second year, which then fruit in the third season.

Under some conditions and, in particular, with some cultivars, this pattern is broken. In place of the lateral vegetative bud, blossoms and fruit can develop on this 1-year-old wood instead of shoots and spurs.

Rome Beauty falls in this category, as do Golden Delicious and Gala. These lateral blossoms characteristically open somewhat later in the spring than terminal blossoms, are smaller, and develop smaller, lower quality fruit.

The length of the shoot and the development of the terminal blossom bud is closely associated with vigor. While the absolute length differs between cultivars and with conditions, shoots over 10 to 12 inches in length are less likely to set a terminal blossom bud. The most fruitful are the shorter shoots called spurs.

In contrast, stone fruits tend to have simple buds, either flower or leaf buds, on 1-year-old wood. The typical pattern is shoot growth one season and flowering from lateral buds on that shoot in the second season. Individual stone fruit species differ in their fruiting habit in that some are more productive on spurs (cherry, plum) or on long, 1-year-old shoots (peach, nectarine).

The growth habit

Within apples, and even within a cultivar or strain, there are important differences in the degree of vegetative growth, spur development, and precocity (age of bearing). These factors are certainly influenced by horticultural practices, such as training (limb bending) and pruning (amount of heading), nutrition management, irrigation, rootstock choice, and thinning program. Aside from the influence of horticultural practices, basic differences in the growth pattern or habit of apple cultivars exist. Recognition of these differences will aid the grower in knowing how to prune a certain cultivar.

For the purpose of this discussion, there are three growth habits that apply to apple. The first one is that shown by spur Delicious. Generally, a spur type of growth habit has a basitonic habit, that is, the bottom part of the tree grows more strongly than the top. The overall tree shape tends to be upright and conical. The leader does not dominate the branching pattern. Most of the fruiting spurs are located on branches 2-years-old or older; spurs continue to be produced on older wood.

Golden Delicious exemplifies the second type of growth habit. The leader dominates the tree's branching pattern. Branches tend to grow at a wide angle (60 to 90 degrees) to the trunk, which enhances fruitfulness. The overall tree shape tends to be spreading, particularly as the fruiting zone moves away

4

from the center of the tree. The fruiting wood consists of a combination of spurs and short shoots.

Rome Beauty is an example of the third type of growth habit, which is generally referred to as a "tip" bearer. The tree shows an acrotonic tendency, which means that branching tends to dominate the upper third of the tree. The tree develops a cylindrical appearance. The fruiting zone rapidly moves toward the outside of the tree. The majority of the spurs are located on 1-and 2-year-old wood, either in a terminal position or in a lateral position on short shoots. The tendency to flower on the ends of long, 1-year-old shoots is the reason for the term "tip" bearer.

FIGURE 1. The growth habit of Golden Delicious (left) and spur-type Delicious (right) is different. Spur-type trees have a greater tendency to grow short spurs rather than shoots. Also, the distance between the spurs is often shorter than in non-spurs such as Golden Delicious.

Each of these different growth types will respond differently to pruning and training. The same type of practice will cause a similar response (i.e., heading into 1-year-old wood will stimulate lateral branches); however, the degree of the response varies widely among cultivars.

Apical dominance phenomenon

Apical dominance is the tendency of a terminal bud, or the resulting actively growing shoot tip and young expanding leaves, to suppress the growth of lateral, lower buds on the shoot. Thus, the frequency of branching is controlled,

FIGURE 2a, b. When branches are growing in a more upright position (2a), they exhibit strong apical dominance. Consequently, spreaders (2b) and other means need to be used to put branches in a more horizontal and fruitful position.

6

and lateral branches that do develop are often less vigorous than the main branch, or are modified in their form.

The role of hormones in controlling tree growth is evident in the phenomenon of apical dominance. Actively growing shoot tips, including young, expanding leaves, are a source of a hormone called auxin. Auxin moves downward with the direction of gravity, inhibiting the growth of lower buds.

The mechanism of the inhibition is not fully understood. Some horticulturists believe that hormones from the tip of the shoot or growing point may act directly to slow or prevent cell division and growth of the dormant buds. Others think that hormones act in some way upon the transport tissues to channel food materials to the tip and away from the lateral buds.

3 WAYS TO AFFECT APICAL DOMINANCE

There are three ways that apple growers can affect the influence of apical dominance upon an apple tree:

1) Remove the auxin source;
2) Spread or tie branches; and
3) Apply chemical growth regulators.

Removing the auxin source   The most direct way in which to affect apical dominance is to remove the shoot tip. This temporarily removes the source of the growth-controlling hormone until a lower shoot assumes dominance. This explains the resulting lateral branching after removing a shoot tip.

Branch spreading and bending   Since auxin moves downward through the plant under the influence of gravity, moving a branch from a vertical position to a more horizontal angle means less hormone is moving down from the tip to affect lower buds and shoots. Consequently, apical dominance is reduced, and lateral branching is more likely to occur. Moving the branch to a position beyond the horizontal completely removes any apical dominance. In this case, a new dominant shoot will arise from the highest point on the spread branch.

Controlling apical dominance may direct enough energy, into otherwise very weak or latent buds, sufficient for the growth of a spur and fruit bud. In higher density orchards, branch spreading to remove apical dominance takes on added importance, because of its effectiveness in making branches more productive and reducing terminal growth. Terminal growth is reduced by the redirection of energy into lateral shoots and fruit production.

Chemical control of apical dominance Certain chemicals, including plant growth regulators, can reduce apical dominance by affecting the auxin relationships within the plant. Chemicals, particularly growth inhibitors, are sometimes used in conjunction with pruning and training in tree management.

The pruning
cut Pruning maintains balance between the vegetative and fruiting portions of the tree. Pruning can determine when a tree comes into bearing and how productive it will remain. Pruning is also considered an overall dwarfing process, because potential growing points are removed. Although certain pruning cuts may increase vegetative growth in the vicinity of the cut, the end result is that the total amount of tree growth will be less. All pruning cuts can be classified into the following categories:

1) Heading into 1-year-old wood;
2) Heading into older wood; and
3) Thinning or "thinning out."

Heading is sometimes referred to as "heading back," especially if the cut is either made at planting or into 1-year-old wood. Heading is readily distinguished from thinning; thinning cuts **always** remove a branch at its origin, that is, the entire shoot or branch is removed. Heading, in contrast, ranges from light tipping to severe pruning into older wood. Thinning is used to remove growth either during dormant or summer pruning,

FIGURE 3a, b, c, d. Figure 3a shows a 1-year-old dormant terminal shoot before a heading cut. Figure 3b shows the same shoot after a heading cut has been made into the 1-year-old wood. This type of cut will stimulate more vigorous growth from lateral buds below the pruning cut and stiffen the branch.

A heading cut next to a spur on weak side shoot (Figures 3c, d) in 2-year-old or older woods is used to shorten branches with the minimum of regrowth.

whereas heading cuts are normally made only during dormant pruning (especially heading into 1-year-old wood).

HEADING INTO 1-YEAR-OLD WOOD

This type of cut is used to stimulate lateral branching where desired or encourage vegetative growth. Heading back is also used during tree establishment. When whips are planted, they are generally headed to force lateral growth. As a result of this invigoration, fruit bud formation is generally discouraged.

Heading into 1-year-old wood on scaffold branches increases the stiffness of the headed branch and thus can be an important part of tree training when establishing the framework for a larger tree.

HEADING INTO OLDER WOOD

There are several categories of heading cuts that fall into this general classification. One of them is a "bench" cut, where the terminal portion of a branch is removed to an outward growing lateral. Bench cuts are generally not recommended for apple trees, as the resulting limb junction is not strong.

Another familiar heading cut is that of limb "shortening." When a branch exceeds its allotted space, or is bending downward from cropping, the terminal portion of that branch is removed to a weak or fruiting lateral. Limb shortening is a critical component of tree training systems such as the slender spindle and vertical axis.

Replacement leader selection is a type of heading also. This type of heading cut involves removing the terminal portion of the leader to a lateral on older (2-year-old-plus) wood. Slender spindle-trained trees use this type of heading to control the leader's vigor.

10

THINNING OUT CUTS

Thinning out cuts remove entire shoots or branches at their place of origin. Thinning is used to open up the tree's canopy, if shading is a problem, especially at the top of the tree. This type of cut is also used in scaffold selection, particularly in the case of too many scaffolds in the lower portion of the tree.

A special cut, called "stubbing," falls into the thinning category. Instead of removing a branch flush to the leader, a small stub (about 1 inch) is left. Adventitious buds then grow and a replacement branch is selected. Stubbing is used extensively in training systems, such as the slender spindle and vertical axis, where fruiting branches are regularly replaced in the upper two-thirds of the tree canopy.

Summary   Training and pruning is often the single most costly and important job in the orchard. It affects when trees start bearing fruit, and directly affects fruit quality.

To prune correctly, pruners must understand the fruiting habit and apical dominance. The fruiting habit of apples and pears is shoot growth the first year, side spur development the second year, and fruit bearing the third year. Apical dominance means the tip of a growing shoot produces a hormone which limits growth of side shoots on that branch below the tip.

Branch spreading and bending is used to modify the effect of apical dominance. The response of a tree to pruning is partly determined by the type of pruning cut that is made. Heading cuts and thinning cuts both use the trees' fruiting and growth habit and apical dominance to control where branches form, how the tree is shaped, and when it bears fruit.

An understanding of pruning principles is the first step in the successful management of trees under high density.

Additional reading

Feucht, W. 1976. Fruitfulness in pome and stone fruits. Washington State University Extension Bulletin, EB 665.

Lespinasse, J.M. 1981. Apple tree management in flat, vertical axis and palmette forms, by cultivar fruiting type. Experiments with other species: plum, peach, pear, and cherry. in; Perspectives de l'horticulture abres fruitiers et petits fruits. *Colloques Scientifiques*, Les Floralies Internationales de Montreal 15:27-130.

Mika, A. 1986. Physiological responses of fruit trees to pruning. *Horticultural Reviews*, Volume 8.

Peterson, A.B. 1979. Projecting production and apple quality from tree inventories. M.S. Thesis, Washington State University, Pullman, Washington. pp.5-7.

Peterson, B. 1985. Pruning Apples: basic concepts. Washington State University Extension Video No. VT 0001.

Wilson, C.L., et al. 1971. Botany. Holt, Rinehart and Winston, New York, N.Y. pp. 31-32.

2 PHYSIOLOGICAL ASPECTS OF PRUNING AND TRAINING

By Curt R. Rom

THE OBJECTIVE OF FRUIT TREE TRAINING SYSTEMS IS TO ENCOURAGE fruit production early and annually throughout the life of the orchard on an efficient and cost-effective basis. All systems have several common elements of tree training and pruning employed to varying degrees to achieve the individual goals of each system. These techniques may result in varied responses, depending upon the timing and degrees to which they are used. The purpose of this chapter is to review some of the elements of training and pruning and a physiological basis for their response. Once a horticulturist understands the basis for the orchard practice, the techniques may be more appropriately employed.

Tree training is the manipulation of growth into the appropriate direction and type of growth desired by the orchard manager. Training is a continuous process of tree management beginning during orchard planning and orchard systems selection, in the early establishment years of the orchard and throughout the life of the orchard to maintain quality fruit production. Pruning, as one element of tree training, is the physical removal of parts of the tree to influence growth, affect flowering, regulate crop load and tree vigor, affect fruit quality, contain tree size, and encourage light penetration into and throughout the canopy. Goals of tree training and pruning include producing a supporting framework for the tree, allowing annual flower formation, developing a tree which allows maximum fruit growth and quality development, and having ease of management access for pruning, thinning, pest control, and fruit harvest.

The elements of tree training systems include: tree genetic system (a rootstock and scion cultivar), tree stock quality and planting, tree support, limb positioning, scoring, pruning, cropping, and use of growth hormones. Several of these topics are discussed in this chapter and throughout the rest of the book. Aspects of pruning and training have been discussed in other reviews and should be used for further reference.

14

The genetic system

Fruit trees are commonly a compound genetic system comprised of a rootstock and a scion cultivar. There are, however, variations of this, including trees which may be grown on their own roots either from cuttings of tissue culture or trees with interstock pieces between the rootstock and scion. Other variations of the compound genetic tree include trees with pollenizer branches grafted onto the tree or novelty trees which have two or more cultivars on the tree frame.

Rootstocks are a key component of the tree training system affecting the tree's adaptability to soils and tolerance of soil stresses (i.e., flooding and drought). Rootstocks control tree size, precocity, and productive potential. The amount of size control imparted by the rootstock will affect elements of the training system, such as tree planting density (trees per acre), the necessity of tree support, amount of support needed for the crop load, pruning requirements, and other management activities such as thinning, harvesting, and spraying for pest control. Selection of the rootstock is critical and should be thoroughly considered as part of the orchard planning process. Rootstock selection will be discussed in a subsequent chapter *(see Chapter 5)*.

Management of the genetic tree The management of the compound genetic tree can modify tree growth and performance and subsequent tree training. Typically, the degree of size control imparted by a rootstock will increase with the amount of the rootstock shank which is above the soil. Some rootstocks form burr knots in aerial exposed shanks. The burr knots are caused by a proliferation of root initials forming at old leaf scars or buds and are characteristic of some stocks (M 26, M 106, etc.). Burr knots may enlarge and cause disruption of the conductive tissue of the tree, causing uneven tree growth and cropping, and may ultimately functionally girdle the tree.

Deep planting of the rootstock shank prevents aerial burr knots and may provide better tree stability, especially against winds, during the early life of a tree. If the graft union of the tree is planted below the soil line, the scion may form roots, and the size-controlling nature and precocious character of the rootstock may be lost. If the height of the graft union above the soil line varies within the orchard, so will tree height, spread, and cropping. Uniform planting depth is required for most uniform tree growth and optimizing tree training.

Trees with dwarfing interstocks (interstems) are often characterized by a degree of size control, precocity, and lateral branch formation with naturally wide angles. The amount of dwarfing imposed by an interstock is characteristic of the clonal material used and the length of the interstem piece. Generally, as the interstem piece increases, tree size will be reduced. Large variation in interstem length will result in a lack of uniformity in tree growth.

Each scion cultivar has a specific growth habit, bearing pattern, and ultimate maximum size. The growth habit of cultivars can be grouped as spur types, non-spur types, terminal bearers, and intermediates. Cultivar can influence tree size on any given rootstock. Some scion cultivars form lateral branches readily, with wide crotch angles (e.g., Gala, Jonagold), while others may have limited lateral branching, shorter lateral shoots, and form a large number of spurs (e.g., Redchief Delicious). Different tree growth habits will greatly influence the need for limb positioning and pruning to stimulate lateral growth. Along with selecting the scion cultivar for its fruit quality characteristics, the orchardist should also consider its growth habit, as it will impact the necessity for tree support, how the tree is pruned, and suitable crop load, etc.

Tree support systems

Two general types of tree support are used in orchard systems. These are:

1) Freestanding trees where the tree trunk provides the vertical support and limbs provide the crop-bearing support, and

2) mechanical support where a post or trellis system substitute for the tree framework and are provided by the orchardist to carry the weight of the tree and crop.

Many dwarfing rootstocks and high density systems require tree support. Some rootstocks have brittle roots (e.g., M 9 or M 26) and/or brittle graft unions (M 26 or Mark). Many of the superior dwarfing stocks are very precocious, bearing fruit during the first or second year in the orchard and productive with heavy yields. Modern orchard systems encourage early cropping and maximum crop loads per tree. Tree support is necessary to support the crop weight without damage to the tree.

Depending upon the rootstock/scion combination, tree quality at planting, and the training system used, trees may require different levels of support; trunk support of 1 meter height (3 feet), complete central leader support with a post or pole 1.75 to 3 meters in height (5-10 feet), or whole tree support with a pole, post, or trellis. The mechanical support required and used in some training systems also provides additional training advantages. Using the support system, limbs can be tied into proper position to encourage fruiting or support a large crop without breakage.

Short trunk support, 1 meter height (3 feet.), will reduce tree leaning, blow-overs, and breakage at the graft union or roots. These supports can often be removed when the tree is mature, although it is often necessary they remain in place. Short trunk supports have limited effect on tree growth and production.

Tall support, 1.5 to 3 meters in height (4½-10 feet), to which the central leader is tied or attached, or whole tree support, allows the central leader to grow rapidly upwards, provides protection from wind movement, prevents tree leaning, blow-overs, and graft union breakage, and allows the tree to crop early in its orchard life. Some of the crop can be grown along the central leader without problems of the central leader bending over, loss of the central leader, or breakage. This is a distinct advantage of supported compared to non-supported trees and can help in the economic return of the cost of the support system.

Supporting a tree with a post, pole or wire has several impacts on the tree. Most notably, the reduction of movement and vibration from wind or load stresses from the crop will reduce the secondary thickening of the trunk xylem and result in trees of small diameter. Studies have shown that within the first several years of growth, staked trees may grow 15 to 25 percent taller and will have 30 to 50 percent smaller trunks. It has also been reported that staked trees may have more branches and longer individual branches. With increased canopy development, light interception will be increased and thus cropping increased *(see next chapter)*.

The possible physiological cause of the increase in trunk diameter to movement is attributed to the production of the gaseous plant hormone, ethylene. Ethylene is typically produced in response to wounds or stresses. Movement and vibration caused by wind or loads cause minute damage to cells and trunk tissue. Consequently, ethylene is produced, and, in response, cell wall development and thickening occurs. Applying an ethylene-generating chemical to plants will cause an increase in stem and trunk diameter.

Staking may influence root growth as well as the aerial por-

18

FIGURE 1. A bamboo post is used to train a young tree in a French axis training system. The bamboo is attached to a wire at a height of 10 feet and attached to the tree trunk. (Jonagold/M 9.)

tions of the tree. Research with landscape trees indicates that supported trees develop smaller root systems. Conversely, reducing wind movement of the tree during tree establishment may encourage new root development along the rootstock. Trees which have been high-budded in the nursery and have a shank extending 10 to 20 centimeters (5-10 inches) when planted with the bud union 2 to 5 centimeters (1-2 inches) above the ground, will need to develop new lateral roots along the shank. Wind movement during the first or second season in the orchard may cause the tree to form a vee-shaped well around the shank inhibiting new root development. Spur cultivars have less early root establishment along the rootstock shank and this will extenuate a wind movement problem. Although conclusive data is not available, it is believed that staking, thereby reducing wind movement and welling around the shank, may improve shank root development and allow early root establishment.

Tree support is necessary at planting for early tree training and maximum growth and cropping response. With support, the tree is allowed to attain its maximum size rapidly and form branches without the need for pruning. No horticultural advantage is apparent for delaying the installation of a support system. Trees or orchard systems requiring support should have them in place at the time of planting. The length of time that tree support is necessary is not clear. In some cases, they can be removed when the tree has filled its space. However, with some rootstocks, and in some training systems, the support remains for the life of the orchard.

Importance of limb positioning

Limb positioning is an aspect of tree training which provides strength to the tree framework, encourages flower formation and cropping, allows for light penetration into the interior of the canopy, and directs growth for balance within the tree.

The proper limb angle gives structural strength to the tree. Narrow crotch angles are structurally weak, often have bark inclusions, and are susceptible to pests and winter injury. Because of the structural weakness associated with narrow angles, limb breakage from wind or crop loads can occur. Limbs with wider crotch angles have greater connective strength, will not break, and will form supporting wood on the underside of limbs to support crop loads. The degree to which limbs are bent or positioned, and the time of year during which positioning is done, affect their growth and cropping.

Each cultivar has a characteristic natural limb angle. Likewise, each form of growth habit requires a different degree of bending to maximize cropping. Regardless of growth habit, as limbs are bent or repositioned from a vertical, upright orientation to a more horizontal orientation, terminal extension growth is reduced, apical dominance is reduced, and lateral branch development is increased.

Limbs can be bent or positioned in two ways. First, the entire limb axis is repositioned to the same angle. This results in a uniform growth response along the length of the limb and a strong crotch angle. The closer to the horizontal a limb is positioned, the more uniform the bud development along the limb and toward the base of the limb. The second bending is an arc bending, where the tip of the limb is bent below some point along the limb, forming an arched or curved limb. Arching limbs creates a different response than straight axis positioning. Arching has little effect on limb crotch angle. At the highest point along the arch, a shoot will typically form. (It will be the longest branch along the limb, and the branch length of other shoots will decrease in both directions from the apex of the arch toward the trunk or the limb tip.) Elongation of the limb terminal will typically stop if the terminal bud is lower than other points along the limb.

Spur-type cultivars (e.g., spur type Delicious) require positioning of 45 to 60 degrees from the vertical for maximum balance of spur formation and lateral shoot growth. Bending limbs below 60 degrees will result in vigorous upright shoot (watersprout) formation. Limbs bent only 30 degrees from the vertical will not adequately form lateral shoots, but only spurs will form at each node.

Naturally branching cultivars (e.g., Golden Delicious, Jonagold, Gala) will develop a good balance between fruiting spurs and lateral branches when spread 60 degrees from the vertical and below. They will not, in many instances, form vigorous watersprouts.

Terminal-bearing cultivars, such as Granny Smith, will naturally bend below the horizontal under the weight of a fruit crop and remain productive. Both of the last two groups of cultivars can have limbs trained to the horizontal to encourage fruiting and control growth. However, bending limbs completely flat (horizontal) will stop terminal growth and stunt scaffold limbs. Limbs and spurs which are pendant and point downward may produce smaller fruit, especially towards the terminal end of the downward hanging shoot.

Little is known about the optimum time of limb positioning, and thorough, quantitative studies of this important issue have not been conducted. Observations indicate bending at different times of the year may result in different immediate responses, although long-term responses may be similar. For example, if limb positioning is done to control vegetative extension growth, bending in late summer after terminal bud formation will not have an effect on either terminal growth or lateral growth for the remainder of that season. However, ultimately, lower limb angles will reduce terminal growth.

If limbs are to be positioned in order to improve flower formation, positioning after flower formation (late summer, fall, or during the dormant season) will not effect flowering in the immediate following season but may in following years. Preliminary experiments have shown that positioning limbs in March, prior to bud break, reduced fruit set of flowers which were on the limb. But two years after bending, there was no difference between various times of bending for flower number and fruit set.

The physiological effect of limb positioning is related to several possible hormone-controlled mechanisms. First, at the time of bending, cell and tissue damage caused by the bending or positioning will result in the release of ethylene. Ethylene causes an increase in limb diameter growth, and a reduction in terminal growth. Ethylene also causes lateral bud development and bud break, resulting in branches or spurs. Research has demonstrated that ethylene is released rapidly after bending limbs of apple trees, but it is dissipated quickly.

Reorientation of the shoot terminal bud also affects shoot apical dominance. In the shoot terminal meristem, the hormone, auxin, is produced. Auxin moves downward in shoots in response to gravity and is partially responsible for inhibition of lateral bud development and branching. When the shoot terminal is bent or repositioned to a more horizontal angle, there is a reduction in terminal extension and thus a quantitative reduction in auxin produced. Since auxins move in response to gravity, they will not be uniformly concentrated throughout the circumference of the limb but will travel along the underside of the limb. Consequently, nodes along the side or top of the limb will be released from apical dominance and begin growth, while those along the bottom of the limb will be inhibited, forming short, weak spurs, or not develop at all.

Many methods can be used to position limbs. On young trees, training for proper limb angles should begin early to encourage strong structural development. When new lateral branches are forming on 1- or 2-year-old wood, clothespins may be attached. Clothespins (spring type) are clamped to the main shoot above the newly forming lateral branch when it is 2 to 5 centimeters (1-2 inches) long. The length of the clothespin will direct the new branch to a more horizontal angle and aid in developing a stronger crotch angle. The clothespins can be removed 4 to 6 weeks later in mid summer.

FIGURE 2a. Clip clothespins are attached to the central leader of a young tree to aid in developing proper crotch angles. Clothespins are attached when new lateral branches are 2.5 to 4 cm long.

Similarly, sturdy wood toothpicks can be used as a very inexpensive tool for developing proper limb angles and strong crotches. Toothpicks should be placed between the main upright shoot and the developing branch when the new branch is 5 to 10 centimeters (2-4 inches) long. Both clothespins and toothpicks are very good tools for establishing good limb crotch angles, but without continued limb positioning with age, the limb angle may be lost, and it will begin to grow upright.

On limbs 1 to 2 years of age, other techniques can be used. Small weights can be hung on the limb to pull the limb to the proper angle. Weights should be placed on the limbs early in the spring, prior to bud break, as wood begins to "soften." Weights

FIGURE 2b. Clothespins are left attached to the central leader until mid summer, when shoots have lignified and will maintain proper crotch angle.

should be left on limbs until lignification of new tissue has occurred, which is mid to late summer. Several problems are inherent with the use of weights. First, using weights to attain proper limb position does not affect limb crotch angle. If poor

FIGURE 3 Toothpicks are used for early limb positioning in apple. Toothpicks are inserted when shoots are 15 cm long, for the primary purpose of developing proper crotch angles of the limbs.

26

angles are developed when the branch is young, it will remain structurally weak and may break due to the weights.

Limbs are often weighted to the desired final angle when the weights are attached. However, the limbs may move to lower angles with time, due to the constant weight. Thus, after weighting, limb angle becomes too low. To the contrary, weights are often removed prior to lignification and hardening of the wood tissue, limbs move back upward, and good limb position is lost.

Improper positioning of weights may cause the limb tip to

FIGURE 4. Small concrete weights can be used to aid in limb positioning on 1- to 3-year-old branches. Weights are clipped onto the limb in early spring and left in place until mid summer. The appropriate angle is achieved by using weights of various weights or in combination.

bend, forming a limb arch. Thus, the tip may be too low, resulting in complete inhibition of growth and the formation of watersprouts. Also, proper limb angle is not achieved. It is best to place weights in the lower half of the limb's length to achieve the

FIGURE 5. String can be used to position limbs to the appropriate angle. String is attached to either the tree trunk or the tree post and then tied to the limbs which require positioning. Limbs are positioned in the spring, and string can be removed in mid summer. String can also be used to tie up limbs with fruit to prevent limb breakage or hanging into dirt or grass.

FIGURE 6. Wooden limb spreaders are used to position limbs on older trees. Spreaders have nails in each end, with one end attached to the tree's central leader and the other into a midsection of the scaffold limb to achieve the appropriate angle.

proper limb angle. Lastly, weights are clipped on limbs with clothespins or tied on with wires. In heavy winds, the weights may pendulum and cause a girdling of the limb.

Limbs may be positioned by using string ties. Strings are looped around the limb and attached to the tree trunk, training post, or trellis wire. Timing of tying depends upon desired response, but is typically done in the spring, and strings are left in place for several months. Similar to using weights, common problems are tying limbs too close to the tip, causing limb arching. Improper knot tying will result in slips, which cause a loss of proper limb angle or a girdling of the limb.

For older, thicker limbs, spreaders are used to position limbs and maintain good angles. Spreaders can be used with limbs of most ages. Spreaders generally reorient the complete limb axis with little chance of arching.

Pruning for tree training

Pruning apple trees is done to accomplish the management objectives of tree training. Pruning can limit tree size, improve light penetration, stimulate lateral branch development, balance shoot and spur development, and limit crop size, thereby improving fruit quality and size, and remove damaged or diseased wood. Pruning can be done almost any time of the year, although response to pruning varies with the time in which it is done.

VEGETATIVE RESPONSE

Pruning is generally considered a dwarfing process, regardless of the time of year during which pruning is done or whether it is branch pruning or root pruning. Pruning causes a dwarfing

30

effect by creating an imbalance of shoot and root growth. It is thought that trees grow with a "functional equilibrium;" shoots and roots grow in proportion to each other to their genetic limits and limits by environmental conditions (soil, moisture, temperature, and nutrition). Pruning disturbs the equilibrium.

For example, pruning and removing shoots results in an imbalance of roots to the remaining shoots. In response, root growth will stop until the balance is re-established. As a result of reduced root growth, there will be a reduction in water and nutrition uptake, and, ultimately, shoot growth will be somewhat reduced. Eventually, the theoretical balance will be regained.

The size controlling effect of pruning has also been explained with a model which has endogenous hormones as the controller of growth. Removing shoots, whereby shoot meristems, terminal, and lateral buds are removed, results in a reduction in auxin production. Auxins are transported basipetally to the root system and cause root branching and development. Roots are the source site of another hormone, cytokinins, which are transported (acropetally) to shoot tips in the transpiration stream of the xylem. Cytokinins are important in cell division and are responsible for bud break and tissue development. Therefore, pruning reduces auxin, which in turn would slow root development. Because of reduced root development, cytokinin production would be limited, and shoot development ultimately would be reduced.

Pruning will reduce total leaf area of the tree canopy. With less leaf area, less total carbohydrate is produced by the tree from photosynthesis. The carbohydrates are transported to storage tissues of the tree and, primarily, the roots. Because of the limited supply of carbohydrates, root growth is reduced, as is the ability to assimilate mineral elements and absorb water. Additionally, respiratory energy from the carbohydrate metabolism is necessary for the active uptake of some minerals and manufacture of key metabolic compounds. These activities may be reduced with limited carbohydrate supplies. With a reduction in mineral element assimilation and reduced potential for the uptake of water, tree growth is reduced.

Although pruning is a dwarfing process, and many studies have shown that total dry matter production by fruit trees is reduced, pruning can have a localized stimulating effect on growth. After pruning a tree, the individual shoots which grow in the following season may be longer than if the tree had not been pruned. After heading back pruning, there are typically more lateral branches formed per shoot than on an unpruned limb. However, total shoot length is reduced. The increase in lateral branch development is due to the removal of the apical meristem, the source of auxin, and apical dominance.

Cytokinin concentration in shoots is increased in early spring after pruning. With the meristem removed and with available cytokinins, other buds develop and form new shoots. The most apical shoot will soon re-establish apical dominance. This is supported by the observation that the most apical new shoot will be the longest, and length of each lower shoot will be shorter. Each additional terminal meristem inhibits the growth of the shoot below.

The localized invigoration phenomena can be partially explained by other factors as well. First, pruning reduces the number of growing points on the tree, and the remaining growing points are supported by the same root system and stored assimilates. Secondly, fruit number is reduced by pruning. and there is less competition between vegetative and fruiting structures for minerals and carbohydrates.

After dormant pruning, soluble carbohydrate and nitrogen levels in wood and developing tissue are higher in the spring and early summer compared to an unpruned tree. Presumably, this is due to the dilution of carbohydrates and nitrogen in the unpruned tree, which has a larger biomass to support with stored carbohydrates from root, young xylem, bark, and other storage tissues. Because of the increase in soluble carbohydrates and nitrogen, shoot vigor of the shoots remaining on a pruned tree is increased, and shoot length and duration of growth are increased. The transport of carbohydrate to the root system for storage in mid to late summer is delayed in pruned trees. By autumn, however, pruned and unpruned trees have similar storage carbohydrate levels.

A second cause of the increase of individual shoot lengths is because of the reduction in crop size (fruit number). Pruning removes a number of flower buds. Fruits are a strong sink for photosynthetically-produced carbohydrates, and their growth can account for 20 to 35 percent of the total tree dry matter accumulation in a growing season. Reducing crop size by pruning will allow more carbohydrates to be partitioned into shoot growth. Similarly, the remaining fruit after pruning will be larger.

Regrowth after pruning is dependent upon tree or limb vigor, the type of cut (heading cuts versus thinning cuts), season of pruning, severity of pruning, and crop load on the tree. The length of new shoots after pruning is correlated to the length or diameter of the shoot which was cut. Generally, heading-back pruning cuts are more stimulating than thinning cuts. After heading, the most terminal shoot on the branch will create apical dominance over the subordinate limbs and grow longer. Thinning cuts, removing lateral branches or adjacent branches, is much less invigorating. Thinning cuts do not change the apical dominance scheme on a limb, and all limbs tend to grow more uniformly.

Pruning severity affects regrowth. The amount of regrowth is somewhat proportional to the amount of wood removed. But, numerous small cuts will result in more regrowth than will a few large cuts, even if the same amount of wood is removed. Heading cuts into the center third of a current season shoot will result in the greatest length of the new apically dominant shoot. Heading cuts by only tipping a shoot will result in shorter regrowth, as will heading into the base of the current season shoot. Heading into older wood will diminish the regrowth response, both in the number of shoots forming from pruning and the length of individual shoots.

Typically, pruning during the dormant season, prior to bud swell, will result in the greatest regrowth response. Pruning after buds swell and flowers develop will reduce the regrowth response. Similarly, pruning during the summer will result in less regrowth than an equal amount of dormant pruning during a single year. However, one or two years after the pruning, whole tree response may be similar. Pruning in late summer or early fall may not result in any regrowth, because buds have entered physiologically-controlled dormancy (rest). Although pruning in the fall or early winter results in no immediate visible growth, it does increase some physiological activity in the buds, making the tree susceptible to early winter injury.

Pruning, then, can be used to control tree size. Pruning will limit the size and direct the shape of the tree. However, on trees which are heavily spurred or spur-bound and carry heavy annual crops, pruning and reducing the crop load may cause an invigoration of the tree and development of younger wood.

Heavily spurred trees have strong apical dominance, many growing points, and heavy crop loads. Pruning to reduce these factors can stimulate regrowth and vegetative extension. (The reduction of crop load is very important, and additional fruit thinning is often necessary to stimulate growth.) Detailed spur pruning has not been successful in stimulating strong vegetative growth. However, spur pruning in combination with heading into 1- or 2-year-old limb sections may stimulate more regrowth.

Thus, although pruning is a "dwarfing" process, using appropriate techniques in the type and severity of pruning can lead to tree size management. Trees which are too large for their allotted orchard space may need pruning for containment. (However, many heading cuts will not achieve this goal.) Trees which are stunted or "runted" by heavy spur formation and cropping, may be invigorated by heaving pruning, with many cuts and spurs removed and a substantial reduction in crop load.

CROPPING EFFECTS

Pruning reduces cropping by limiting both fruit number and total fruit weight. However, fruit quality is generally improved in response. The fruit which remain on the tree are larger and may have improved fruit type. Because pruning can improve light relations in the tree, fruit color and soluble solids may be improved.

Pruning will remove fruit buds at the time of pruning, and, because of the reduction in total tree shoot length, flower bud number for future crops will be reduced proportionally. Because of the invigoration of growth after pruning, fewer of the remaining buds will have time for flower initiation and development to occur during the growing season. Dormant pruning will especially decrease flower formation on young, vigorous trees, trees on vigorous rootstocks, and spur-type cultivars. Heading cuts tend to reduce cropping more than thinning cuts, because of the increase in vegetative lateral bud development. Thus, pruning young trees reduces their precocity and delays their production. In training systems which require early production for economic return to the system and/or to help control tree size and vigor, pruning should be minimized.

In mature trees, the reduction in cropping by pruning is an important part of the fruit thinning program. However, excessive pruning can severely limit yields and cause the trees to become overly vegetative and vigorous.

Pruning may cause a redistribution of flower buds. Because of the location of pruning throughout a tree canopy, the formation of new shoots or spurs and improved light distribution within the canopy, flower buds may be more uniformly distributed.

After dormant pruning, fruit set is generally not affected or may be higher compared to unpruned trees. The fruits which remain on the tree after pruning have reduced competition between fruits for stored assimilates and, given adequate pollination, will develop rapidly and be retained by the tree. However, it has been reported that fruit set may be reduced after heavy pruning, due to increased competition between very vigorous shoots and the developing fruits. Because of the reduction in crop load, the fruits on pruned trees may be larger by harvest. If pruning is done such that light penetration within the canopy is improved, fruit color of red-colored cultivars is improved.

Conversely, fruit quality can also be negatively impacted by pruning. After severe pruning and subsequent vigorous vegetative regrowth, fruits may have increased incidence of calcium deficiency-related disorders, such as cork spot or pitting. This is due to both the dilution of calcium in large fruits and the preferential partitioning of calcium into vigorous shoot growth early in the season. If pruning causes a dense, closed canopy or a hedged canopy effect, light penetration into the canopy is limited and fruit color development will be limited.

SUMMER PRUNING

Although pruning is commonly done during the dormant season, pruning may be done during the growing season to achieve very specific objectives. These objectives may include removing damaged or diseased wood, to improve light distribution within the tree, to improve fruit quality, and to use available labor during summer.

Like dormant pruning, summer pruning is a dwarfing process. Many of the general responses to dormant pruning apply to summer pruning, although the amount of time between treatment and response is sometimes different. For example, after late summer or early fall pruning, there may be no substantial regrowth. Although the following spring, growth may be similar to pruning done the same dormant season. Pruning done in mid summer may have a similar initial response to dormant pruning, but, because of shortening days and cooling temperatures, shoot regrowth may be reduced.

Early summer pruning is commonly referred to as pinching; removing the terminals of limbs and shoots to stimulate lateral branches and spurs. This is common practice on some strongly apical dominant cultivars, such as spur-type trees and terminal-bearing cultivars, which have a tendency to form blind-wood. Pinching should be done in the first 4 to 6 weeks of the season. In regions where there is a short growing season (less than 180 days), there may be no beneficial influence on flower formation due to pinching in the season after pinching treatments. However, in milder, longer growing seasons, the short branches or spurs which form in response to pinching may set flower buds and fruit the following year.

Summer pruning to remove watersprouts or suckers will improve light distribution to the canopy interior. If done in mid summer, fruit color and return bloom may be improved. Removing these vegetative, "weedy" shoots should be done in early summer for maximum light distribution throughout the season but may require a second treatment due to regrowth.

Summer pruning in mid to late summer may improve fruit color by exposing shaded fruits to sunlight. However, fruits which were shaded for most of the season and then exposed to sunlight are more sensitive to sunburn. Summer pruning may also improve fruit calcium content and firmness. Fruit size and soluble solids, however, may be reduced. These effects are possibly related. Firmness may be improved, due to removal of competitive sinks for calcium or due to reductions in fruit size. Fruit size and soluble solids are reduced by the loss of leaf area. In the last portion of the fruit development period, shoot leaves are important for continued fruit growth.

Flower formation   Summer pruning can reduce flower formation. Similar to dormant pruning, part of the effect is the removal of potential fruit bearing surface. Pruning may also cause a vegetative invigoration of buds and prevent flower bud initiation during the remainder of the season. Severe summer pruning late in the summer or in early fall can cause a "fall bloom;" flower buds initiated for the following season's crop will bloom in the fall and are subsequently lost to production. However, careful summer pruning improves light distribution throughout the canopy and results in improved spur distribution.

After summer pruning, photosynthesis of remaining leaves may increase. However, the increase in carbohydrates in the remaining leaves does not completely compensate for leaves removed by the pruning. Carbohydrates produced by the leaves, and those which previously were being stored as reserves in roots, are used for regrowth. Storage of carbohydrates in the roots for dormant respiration is reduced and delayed.

Summer pruning should be part of a total pruning strategy. Excessive summer pruning, like severe dormant pruning, will reduce cropping potential of the tree.

In conclusion

Training is the total system of horticultural practices necessary to produce an economic crop. The elements of training (genetics, staking, spreading, pruning, and cropping) are interrelated. To practice only one element without considering the impact on the whole system. may lead to poor results. The orchardist cannot consider and practice an individual element of tree training in isolation, but must consider the entire tree training system. Otherwise, the result of a single practice may negate the anticipated outcome of another practice and prevent the orchardist from achieving the system objectives.

The majority of tree training practices are used to improve cropping and economic yield. Using techniques incorrectly, or ignoring the necessity of tree training, can have long-term negative economic consequences. Understanding training elements, and the physiological basis, will aid fruit growers in maximizing the production system.

Additional reading

Abbott, D.L. 1984. *The Apple Tree: physiology and management*. Grower Books, London. 90 pages.

Ferree, D.C. 1981. Physiological aspects of pruning and training. in; Tree Fruit Growth Regulators and Chemical Thinning. Shortcourse Proceedings. 1981. R.B. Tukey, and M.W. Williams, eds. WSU Cooperative Extension publication. p 90-104.

Geissler, D. and D.C. Ferree. 1984. Response of plants to root pruning. Hort Rev. 6:155-188.

Greene, D.W. 1981. Growth regulator and cultural techniques to promote early fruiting of apples. in; Tree Fruit Growth Regulators and Chemical Thinning. Shortcourse Proceedings.

1981. R.B. Tukey, and M.W. Williams, eds. WSU Cooperative Extension publication. p 90-104.

Heinicke, D.L. 1975. High density apple orchards, planning, training, and pruning. USDA Agr. Handbook No. 458. 34 pages.

Jackson, J.E. 1980. Light interception and utilization by orchard systems. Hort. Rev. 2:208-267.

Marini, R.P. and J.A. Barden. 1987. Summer pruning of apple and peach trees. Hort. Rev. 9:351-376.

Mika, A. 1986. Physiological response of fruit trees to pruning. Hort. Rev. 8:339-378.

Perry, R.L. 1989. Tree stakes aid growth. *American Fruit Grower.* 109(3): 54-57.

Rom, C.R. 1985. Bud development and vigor. in; *Pollination and Fruitset Shortcourse Proceedings. Good Fruit Grower.* p 1-17.

Rom, C.R. and B. Peterson. 1985. Summer pruning can yield mixed results. *Good Fruit Grower.* 36(1):12.

Stebbins, R.L. 1980. Training and pruning apple and pear trees. Northwest Ext. Pub. 156. WSU Coop. Ext. Service.

Tukey, H.B. 1964. Dwarfed apple trees. MacMillan and Co., New York. p 316-401.

Ulmer, V.E. 1968. Fruitfulness in pome and stone fruits. Ext. Bul 665. WSU Coop. Ext. Service.

Westwood, M.N. 1978. *Temperate Zone Pomology.* W.H. Freemont and Sons, Inc. 428 pages.

3 LIGHT INTERCEPTION AND UTILIZATION IN ORCHARDS

By Curt R. Rom and Bruce H. Barritt

IN ORCHARDS, ECONOMIC YIELD IS THE PRODUCT OF THE NUMBER OF trees per acre, the number of flowers on each tree, the number of flowers which set fruit, and the ultimate size and quality of the fruit. Maximizing orchard performance, then, means maximizing each of these factors early during the life of the orchard, and annually. Studies have demonstrated that light intercepted by the orchard, and light distribution throughout the tree canopy, relates to flower formation, fruit set, fruit development, and quality. Through tree training and pruning, orchard operators can manipulate the light environment within the canopy and affect orchard efficiency.

This chapter will review orchard light relations in order to develop an understanding of how orchard system design and tree management may be managed to maximize fruit production and quality. Topics which will be addressed are:

1) Why is light important to fruit trees
2) How does light penetration vary within a tree canopy
3) When during the season is light important?

Chapter Four will further discuss relationships between light distribution within a tree and spur and fruit quality development. Together, these chapters and others within this volume provide a basis for management decision-making for tree training.

Why is light important?

Orchard productivity is related to the amount of light intercepted by the orchard. Light interception is the amount (or percentage) of total available light intercepted by the fruit tree canopy, and which does not strike the orchard floor. Interception of 100 percent of available sunlight would indicate that all of the light over an area of orchard is intercepted by the tree leaves with none of the light striking the orchard floor. This level of interception is not practical in most orchard systems because of the need for room between rows or around trees for the operation of equipment and harvesting.

Because fruit trees grow in three dimensions (vertically and two directions horizontally), the tree canopy needs light shining on several canopy surfaces. This need requires space between trees. In fact, research has indicated that, because of these issues, orchard production is maximized at about 70 percent light interception. In modern systems, trees are grown in hedgerows to allow maximum surface exposure with space between the tree rows.

Light interception should be maximized early in the life of the orchard in order to maximize production by the tree. Early light interception is a function of tree density and tree quality at planting. Well-branched nursery trees developed up to 2 square meters (2½ square yards) of leaf area in the first year in the orchard and 6 square meters (7 square yards) in their second year *(Table 1)*. The leaf area developed in the first season of planting was well correlated to the size of the trees at planting but was dependent upon the scion cultivar and rootstock. The amount of light intercepted during the first two seasons was correlated to the leaf area and the size of the canopy. Planting high quality, well-branched nursery trees and increasing tree density increases the leaf area per unit of land area and results in increased light interception.

As trees mature in size and fill their allotted space, the interception of light early in the season is important for early fruit growth and development. The interception of light during the season is a function of the rate of leaf area development. Early in the season, spur leaves are the first leaves to appear on the tree. By bloom, only 20 to 50 percent of the spur leaf area is developed. After bloom, bourse shoots on fruiting spurs begin to grow and add to the leaf area on spurs. During the first one-half or two-thirds of the season, extension shoots develop and add a substantial amount of leaf area to the tree canopy.

On a whole tree basis, fruiting spur leaves comprise 15 to 25 percent of the total canopy leaf area, while nonfruiting and vegetative spurs may comprise 30 to 40 percent of the leaf area.

TABLE 1. Leaf area development in the first year in the orchard of well-branched nursery trees.

| | Leaf Area per Tree (m²) | | | |
| | | Year 2 | | |
Cultivar/Rootstock	Year 1	Spurs	Shoots	Total
Cultivar:				
Jonagold	1.75	.94	4.72	5.66
Delicious	.73	.69	1.97	2.66
Rootstock:				
M 7a	1.13	1.03	3.76	6.70
EMLA 26	1.35	.86	2.94	3.80
Cultivar/Rootstock:				
Jonagold/EMLA 26	1.57	1.18	3.93	5.11
Jonagold/M 7a	1.92	1.22	5.52	6.74
Delicious/EMLA 26	.68	.55	1.95	2.50
Delicious/M 7a	.78	.79	1.98	2.77

Trees planted in eastern Washington State, March 1, 1987. Leaf area measured September 1987 and 1988. Data are averages of 16 trees of the cultivar/rootstock combination.

Shoot leaves comprise approximately 30 to 40 percent of the tree total.

Fruiting spur leaves provide the carbohydrates necessary for initial fruit growth, cell division, and fruit set. After 20 to 40 days after bloom, the spur's leaves are inadequate to maintain fruit growth rate, and bourse shoot leaves and vegetative shoot leaves are important for maintained fruit growth. Shoot leaves produce carbohydrates in excess of that needed by fruits. These carbohydrates are then used for additional shoot and leaf growth, root development, and storage carbohydrates necessary to maintain respiratory needs of the tree during the dormant season and to tolerate stresses (temperature or drought). Vegetative spur leaves also contribute to fruit growth during the middle of the growing season and are important in fruit bud development for the following year. Shading of these leaves during the critical periods of the year will result in reductions in yield and growth activity in the current and succeeding year.

Factors affecting tree vigor and growth, i.e., nutrition, water, temperature, crop load, pest damage, etc., affect light interception early in the season. The goal is to have trees develop a complete canopy as early as possible during the season, but not grow to such an extent as to excessively shade portions of the tree or adjacent trees later in the season.

The structure of the tree itself and other supporting structures (trellises, poles, etc.) will intercept some light whereby light is unavailable to leaves. In large, old trees, an estimated 60 percent of the light can be intercepted by the wood frame of the tree. Less light is intercepted by the frame of younger and smaller trees. The amount of light intercepted by supporting structures has not been well studied but is generally considered to be minimal compared to the tree canopy.

Light distribution within the tree canopy is the next major issue. When light strikes an apple tree leaf, approximately 85 percent of the light is absorbed or reflected by the leaf, and only 15 percent of light energy passes through the leaf. Because of the absorption and reflection of light by leaves, the light energy decreases as it penetrates through a tree canopy. The rate at which it decays is an exponential function of the number of leaves and the thickness of the canopy. Light in tree canopies has been measured in the Pacific Northwest in several types of tree canopies to investigate the rate of light decay. Figure 1 represents the decrease in light energy within a tree canopy as a function of distance from the top or edge of the tree canopy.

The closer to the center or bottom of the tree, the less light is available *(Figure 1) (see Chapter Four)*. Light can travel 1 to 2 meters (3-6 feet) through the tree canopy before light levels are decreased below 30 percent, a lower threshold for maximum physiological activity. Thus, in large, dense tree canopies, light can be limiting for growth and development in almost one-third of the canopy volume.

Light within the canopy controls distribution of mineral elements and carbohydrates. Well-exposed portions of the tree will have leaves with high levels of leaf nitrogen, while shaded portions have lower levels. When leaves are shaded, nitrogen is exported out of the shaded leaves to leaves which are better exposed. Thus, leaves at the top and edge of dense canopies will have higher nitrogen levels and shoots will tend to be more vigorous.

Zinc deficiencies may be disguised by poor light. Leaves and shoots with low zinc, which are formed under low light conditions, may not show deficiency symptoms of small size, narrow shapes, and rosettes, although tissue levels are low. Good light distribution within the canopy will result in more uniform distribution of nitrogen and other elements, along with better distribution of vigor.

Ideally, to maximize light interception and have adequate

light distribution within the canopy, tree canopies should have a large surface area-to-volume ratio. Many high density training systems take advantage of this ratio. Thus, the canopies are often a narrow 1 to 2 meters (3-6 feet), and may extend from 2 to 5 meters (6-18 feet) in height.

Light is important for fruit growth and quality in two basic processes. First, light is necessary for the photosynthetic reaction in leaves. Photosynthesis is the chemical fixation of carbon dioxide from the air into carbohydrates, which can be used by the tree for energy storage, and chemical building blocks used

LIGHT DISTRIBUTION DECREASES WITHIN THE TREE CANOPY

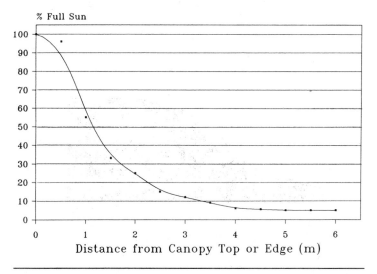

FIGURE 1. Light decreases in energy as it passes through tree canopies. Data in the curve represents data taken from trees of several ages and designs in eastern Washington State.

for wood growth, leaf growth, fruit growth, and fruit sugars. Approximately 30 to 50 percent of full sunlight is necessary for maximum photosynthesis by the leaves *(Figure 2)*. Limiting light (sunlight) by shading within a tree canopy reduces photosynthesis, thereby reducing carbohydrates available for growth. Under reduced carbohydrate supply within a fruit tree, shoot growth, root growth, and mineral uptake are reduced, and flower bud formation, fruit set, and fruit growth are minimized.

Secondly, light is important for color in some fruits, such as Red Delicious apples. The color pigment is formed from carbohydrates manufactured via photosynthesis, but light must also

LIGHT SATURATION FOR APPLE

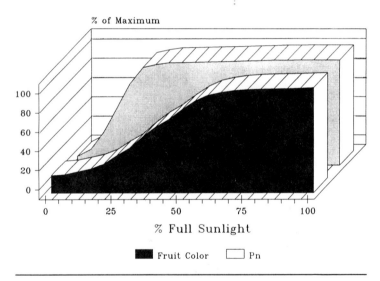

FIGURE 2. The relationship of light to photosynthesis and red color development in apple.

hit the fruit directly to allow the chemical reactions, which create the red anthocyanin pigments, to proceed. Depending upon the specific cultivar, generally 50 to 75 percent full sun is necessary to develop a full, deep, maximum red color *(Figure 2)*.

The effects of limiting light in fruit trees is easily demonstrated by shading studies. Shading apple shoots to levels between 50 and 100 percent ambient sunlight caused only a 5 to 10 percent reduction in photosynthesis. However, shoots grown in 25 percent sunlight had significantly reduced photosynthesis; by about 60 to 70 percent. In an apple tree canopy with natural shade, vegetative watersprouts (suckers) in the center of the tree received only about 25 percent full sunlight *(Table 2)*. Watersprouts were longer than shoots on the canopy periphery but had less leaf area per shoot and lower leaf efficiency (more on leaf efficiency in a Chapter Four). The photosynthetic rate on a leaf area basis was only about one-third of that compared to leaves of a similar age on vegetative shoots on the canopy periphery. On a total shoot basis (photosynthesis per area by total leaf area), shoots in the shaded canopy interior assimilated only a fraction of the carbon that shoots on the canopy exterior assimilated.

The light environment in the tree canopy changes during the season as a result of increased leaf development, movement of limbs by positioning or bending with a crop, or the loss of leaf area due to pests, drought, or summer pruning. Leaves of apple trees will physiologically adapt to changing light conditions in the canopy. Leaves which develop in high light and are subsequently shaded and then reexposed, will have photosynthetic rates lower than leaves continuously exposed to maximum light. Similarly, leaves which develop in shaded conditions and are subsequently exposed to higher light, adapt to the new light environment and will increase in photosynthesis compared to continuously shaded leaves. However, they will not have rates as high as leaves which were continuously exposed to maximum light.

Similarly, for maximum fruit color and quality, fruit must be exposed to optimum light for the entire season. Fruits which are shaded early in the season will not attain the maximum size or color, even if given adequate light later in the season. Fruits which develop in low light and are then exposed to high light are more susceptible to sunburn injury.

The light environment in the tree canopy is not consistent, since light can penetrate as small beams, which are constantly changing in size and location as the sun passes overhead. Because of movement in the wind, leaves can be exposed to high light or low light very rapidly. The plant can adjust its photosynthetic rate rapidly to these conditions; in a matter of seconds. Also, a portion of a leaf may be in shade while another is exposed. Leaves can have different photosynthetic rates occurring on the same leaf simultaneously.

TABLE 2. Light exposure, shoot development, and photosynthesis of two vegetative shoot types in a Delicious apple tree canopy.

| | | | | Photosynthesis | |
| | | | | per area | per shoot |
Type	Light percent full sun	Leaf area/shoot cm^2	Shoot length cm	mg CO2 per dm^2/hr	mg CO2 per shoot/hr
Extension	80	704	43	21	148
Watersprout	23	512	72	6	34

Extension shoots are exposed vegetative shoots on canopy periphery. Watersprouts are shoots of same age growing vertically in canopy interior. Measurements made in mid July.

The leaves in the canopy interior, thus, are relatively efficient at maximizing photosynthesis with the light resources available. However, heavy shading (less than 30% sunlight) for prolonged periods may be detrimental to the ability of the tree to assimilate carbon, produce carbohydrates, and export the carbohydrates throughout the tree for growth and development.

Jackson and Palmer (1977), at the East Malling Research Station, have done some classic studies of the effects of shade on fruit production. When whole trees of Cox's Orange Pippin apple were shaded to levels of 11, 25, and 37 percent, and compared to trees given full sun during an entire season, fruit set was dramatically reduced. Although the fruit which remained on shaded trees were slightly larger than on trees exposed to normal sunlight (not shaded), the total yield per tree was reduced. Shading trees to 25 percent of full sun reduced yield approximately 50 percent compared to the nonshaded trees. More important were the effects of shade the following year.

The year after trees received the shading treatments (and trees were not shaded in the second year), trees which had received less than full sunlight had less flowers, less fruit set, and smaller fruit. Thus, the tree had a "memory" for the light environment, and the detrimental effects of shade carried over to the next year. This demonstrates the importance of light to fruit production and that light management is a continuous operation.

When during the season is light needed?

The light environment within the canopy changes during the season. Light can become limited in interior sections of the canopy very early in the season. Thus, knowledge of when during the year light is most critical in spur development and fruit development is necessary for optimizing tree design and management.

Limbs of Oregon Spur Delicious/M 7 were shaded for an entire season, or various periods during the season, from petal fall until harvest, to evaluate the effects of reduced light early in the season, in mid season, and late season. The shade reduced light distribution to the limbs below 30 percent full sunlight. Spur development and fruit development throughout the season were monitored.

Shade during the entire season or the middle of the season reduced spur leaf number and area of both vegetative and fruiting spurs. Fruiting spur leaf number was reduced by shading, primarily due to a decrease in the number of bourse shoot leaves.

Any period of shading reduced spur leaf efficiency (specific leaf weight). Leaves which were shaded lost leaf nitrogen and

TABLE 3. Shade at different times during the season affects fruit development of Redspur Delicious/M 7.

Treatment[1]	Fruit set	Fruit weight Avg.	Total	Fruit color	Starch rating	Soluble solids
		(Percentage of Control[2])				
Control	100	100	100	100	100	100
0-140 days	55	98	49	86	119	89
0-47 days	54	116	48	100	115	87
47-93 days	101	81	101	96	100	82
93-140 days	95	94	100	92	100	83

[1] *Control is unshaded. Other treatments were given 63 percent shade during the time specified (0 = petal fall, 140 = harvest).*

[2] *All data given as the percentage of the unshaded control.*

had some loss of the photosynthetic pigment, chlorophyll. Shading during the first two-thirds of the season reduced bud diameter of vegetative spurs.

Shade early in the season during the fruit cell division and June-drop period, reduced fruit set dramatically *(Table 3)*. The fruit were nearly similar in size to unshaded fruit by the end of the season, but there was 52 percent reduction in total fruit weight compared to nonshaded controls. Shade during mid season had no effect on fruit set, but, more importantly, reduced final fruit size, color, and soluble solids, even though the fruit had full sunlight for the last 45 days of the season. Shading fruit for the last 47 days of the season dramatically reduced color and soluble solids.

When light is limiting and, presumably, photosynthesis is reduced, the tree balances itself by reducing crop load via fewer flowers and reduced fruit set. Thus, reduced light (shade) limits total crop weight, even though individual fruit size may not be affected. In a subsequent experiment, limbs of all treatments carried the same crop load (fruit number/limb cross sectional area). With crop load being equal, fruit growth of limbs shaded during the first third or middle of the season was reduced. Thus, fruit growth rates were reduced by low light in mid to late part of the season, and fruit size was adversely affected. Shade during the last third of the season had the greatest effect on fruit quality *(Figure 3)*.

Light problems within the canopy can occur very early in the season. However, the exposure of fruit and spurs to adequate light is necessary throughout the entire season. If fruiting spurs are shaded any time from budbreak till June drop, fruit set will be reduced. Although some canopy shading problems can be corrected by mid or late summer pruning, the pruning will only affect the color of the remaining fruit, as it is too late to affect fruit set and early fruit growth rates. Similarly, in some cultivars, flower formation will have occurred by mid summer, and summer pruning to expose limbs to light may be done too late to improve return bloom.

Light within the canopy changes during the day, as does the ability of the tree to utilize the light. Individual leaves will maximize photosynthesis as soon as temperature is appropriate and light is sufficient; usually this occurs within one or two hours of sunrise. The individual leaf will maintain a maximum rate, even though light intensity continues to increase. Under conditions of high temperature and high transpirational demand, as occurs in eastern Washington State in midsummer, the leaf may undergo an incipient water stress due to resistances in water moving

SHADE INFLUENCES FRUIT DEVELOPMENT

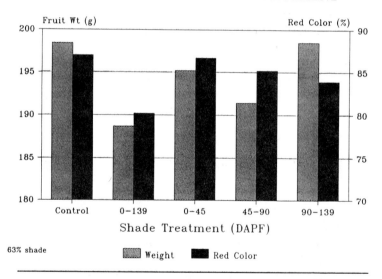

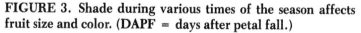

FIGURE 3. Shade during various times of the season affects fruit size and color. (DAPF = days after petal fall.)

54

through the tree. Consequently, photosynthesis will be reduced as stomates close. Under these circumstances, photosynthesis will be maintained at a lower rate or will slowly decrease during the afternoon, until light becomes limiting.

Whole tree photosynthesis is similar to individual leaves in some respects. Whole tree photosynthesis will increase as light intensity increases, but the rate will continue to increase until almost solar noon. As the sun moves directly above the canopy, intercanopy shading occurs, the shaded inner areas of the tree have reduced photosynthesis, and whole tree photosynthesis is reduced. After solar noon, whole tree photosynthesis may increase, as more surface area of the tree is exposed. If the trees are water stressed or if there are high transpirational conditions (low humidity and high temperatures), whole tree photosynthesis will decline. As the sun moves lower in the horizon as the afternoon progresses, whole tree photosynthesis decreases.

Information on the time of day which fruit trees can most efficiently use light for carbohydrate assimilation is limited. Consequently, tree training systems which capitalize on such ideas are also limited.

Managing light in the orchard

Apple growers have the ability to manage the light in their orchard. Light interception and distribution is affected by the orchard design, tree training system, and pruning and training practices.

When designing and planning an orchard, growers ought to consider light and its importance. Tree rows should, if possible, be oriented to maximize light interception. The training system should be selected to accomplish the management objectives of the operation and should be selected to maximize light interception and distribution. Wide trees with a large canopy volume may intercept a high percentage of available light; however, because of poor light distribution within the canopy, economic yield is reduced by lack of flowers, fruit set, and quality. Narrow tree canopies or short trees planted at high densities will maximize light interception and have adequate light distributed throughout the canopy. The important cultivar and rootstock decision and appropriate planting density for the system should consider the role and importance of light *(see Chapter Five)*.

One of the goals of tree training and pruning is to maximize light distribution in order to increase flower development, fruit set, and quality fruit production *(see Chapter Two)*. Limb positioning to angles of 45 or 60 degrees allows light to penetrate into the center of the tree canopy. Light "windows" can be made by spacing scaffold limbs apart by .5 to 1 meter (20-36 inches) or more, and spacing scaffold limbs around the tree for ladder or picking bays. Removing overgrowth in the top of the tree and retaining tree form allows for light to reach lower portions of the tree. Pruning to remove limbs which cross-over, grow toward the canopy interior, or shade other limbs improves light to the remaining fruit-bearing wood. Removing watersprouts and suckers in the canopy interior allows fruiting wood to have adequate light. Summer pruning can expose fruits which were shaded, allowing them to color better, and may improve spur development in the canopy interior.

Nutrition, water, and pest management affect the ability of the tree to utilize light for photosynthesis. Nonvigorous trees stop growth early in the season, thereby leaves "age" early and photosynthesis decreases. Trees low in nitrogen have reduced photosynthetic rates, as well as reduced leaf development. Trees which are water stressed will stop photosynthesis early in the day and not utilize available light. Some pests such as mites and leafhoppers will reduce photosynthesis with heavy populations.

56

Insects which damage the leaves, such as leafminers, leafrollers, and aphids, reduced photosynthetic surface. Thus, with poor or inattentive management, photosynthesis may be reduced, and the production of carbohydrates will limit fruit and tree growth, even with high levels of available light and potential canopy interception.

Production of a large economic crop, i.e., high production and high quality, requires management attention to all aspects of good horticulture. Paramount among management objectives, fruit growers must manage light within the orchard to maximize their crop. Orchard systems must intercept light and have leaves capable of utilizing the light for photosynthesis. Light must be well-distributed throughout the tree for the entire growing season to maximize fruit size and quality.

The research presented in this chapter was funded by the Washington Tree Fruit Research Commission, projects 5640, 5717, and 7294. The authors gratefully acknowledge the support of the Washington fruit growers and orchards where cooperative studies were conducted. Thanks to Bonnie Schonberg and Mark Den Herder for technical assistance in the research.

Additional reading

Barden, J.A. 1978. Apple leaves, their morphology, and photosynthetic potential. *HortScience* 13(6):644-646.

Barritt, B.H. and C.R. Rom. 1987. Management of apple fruiting spurs for fruit quality and profitability. III-V. *Good Fruit Grower* 38(21):58.

Barritt, B.H. and C.R. Rom. 1987. Renovation pruning shapes up central leader trees. *Good Fruit Grower* 38(2):14-18.

Barritt, B.H. and C.R. Rom. 1986. Training and renovation of apple trees. Proc. 82nd Ann. Meeting Wash. State Hort. Assoc. 82:82.

Ferree, D.C. 1984. Managing light in high density orchard systems. Proc. 79th Ann. Meeting, Wash. State Hort. Assoc. 79:129-133.

Ferree, D.C. 1978. Cultural factors influencing net photosynthesis of apple trees. *HortScience* 13(6):650-652.

Jackson, J.E. and J.W. Palmer. 1977. Effect of shade on the growth and cropping of apple trees. II. Effects on components of yield. *J. Hort. Sci.* 52:253-266.

Jackson, J.E. 1980. Light interception and utilization by orchard systems. *Hort. Reviews.* 2:208-267.

Robinson, T.L., E.J. Seeley, B.H. Barritt. 1983. Effect of light environment and spur age on Delicious apple fruit size and quality. *J. Amer. Soc. Hort. Sci.* 108:855-861.

Rom, C.R. 1985. How spur quality influences fruit size. Proc. Wash. State Hort. Assoc. 81:109-118.

Rom, C.R. and B. Peterson. 1986. Summer pruning can yield mixed results. *Good Fruit Grower* 36(1):12.

Rom, C.R. and B.H. Barritt. 1987. Management of apple fruiting spurs for fruit quality and profitability. II. Spur development. *Good Fruit Grower* 38(21):21.

Simpson, J., C.R. Rom, and M.E. Patterson. 1988. Causes and possible controls of sunburn on apples. *Good Fruit Grower* 39(2):16-17.

Ulmer, V.E. 1968. Fruitfulness in pome and stone fruits. Ext. Bul. 665. WSU Coop. Ext. Service.

4 SPUR

QUALITY, LIGHT

MANAGEMENT,

AND RENOVATION

PRUNING

By Bruce H. Barritt and Curt R. Rom

THE GENERAL RULES FOR THE PRODUCTION OF HIGH QUALITY fruit include:

1) Strong fruiting spurs produce fruit of high quality;
2) Sunlight is the critical factor in the production of strong spurs;
3) Pruning is the technique used to ensure adequate sunlight distribution to all parts of the canopy.

In an earlier chapter, we discussed the harmful effects of reduced light levels, shade, on the most critical of physiological processes, photosynthesis. This chapter describes our studies with spur Red Delicious in Washington State that attempt to more fully understand the relationships to fruit quality of spur quality, sunlight level, and renovation pruning.

Apple fruiting spurs

SPUR QUALITY AND CANOPY POSITION

To study the influence of canopy position on spur quality, twelve 17-year-old central leader-trained Oregon Spur Delicious/MM 104 trees were selected in a commercial orchard in Manson, Washington. Tree spacing was 3 by 5.5 meters (10 by 18 feet) and tree height approximatley 4 meters (13 feet). Each tree canopy was divided into thirds, with sampling sites near the central leader at 1, 2, and 3 meters (3.3, 6.5, and 10 feet) above soil level. These locations will be referred to as top, middle, and bottom canopy positions. Spurs and fruit, as well as sunlight levels, were evaluated at harvest time from each location.

Leaf and spur efficiency Apple spurs vary considerably in their number, size, and weight of leaves. These leaf values were measured along with the total leaf area per spur, total leaf dry weight per spur, and specific leaf weight. Leaves growing in the shade are often as large as leaves in full sun, but they are thinner. This means that their weight (mg) per unit area (cm^2), or their specific leaf weight, is lower. **Leaf efficiency** is the term used for specific leaf weight because it is correlated with the rate of photosynthesis, the physiological process or the "factory" in every leaf that produces carbohydrates for fruit and tree growth. **Spur efficiency** is the term used for total leaf dry weight per spur, a measure of the ability of all the leaves on a spur to provide photosynthates for fruit and bud growth. Spur efficiency is a measure of the size of the photosynthetic factory, and leaf efficiency is a measure of the rate of photosynthesis.

Vegetative spurs   These spurs do not have flower clusters in the current season but probably will have flower clusters the next spring. The spurs in the top of the tree have a significantly greater number of leaves, greater leaf area per spur, greater spur efficiency, higher leaf efficiency, and larger bud diameter than spurs in the bottom canopy position *(Table 1)*. Two characteristics of particular importance are leaf and spur efficiency, as they show the greatest reduction from the top to the bottom canopy position, 45 percent and 59 percent, respectively. Reduction in leaf and spur efficiency of this magnitude illustrates the tremendous impact canopy position has on spur quality.

It is obvious that vegetative spurs in the bottom canopy position are not as strong as spurs in the top position and, therefore, are not as likely to be strong flowering spurs the following spring.

Fruiting spurs   In addition to leaves, these spurs support a maturing fruit. Canopy location of fruiting spurs did not influence the number of leaves on a spur or leaf area per spur *(Table 2)*. Each fruiting spur selected for study was sufficiently strong the previous fall to develop a flower cluster and set a fruit, and, therefore, large differences in leaf number the current summer would not be expected. In other words, it can be the growing environment the previous summer that influences spur leaf number the current summer. However, it is the growing environment during the current summer that influences leaf efficiency, spur efficiency, and fruit set *(Table 2)*. Leaf efficiency was reduced 36 percent and spur efficiency 37 percent from the top to bottom canopy position. This trend was also observed with pyramid-shaped Golden Delicious trees in Ohio, where leaf efficiency was reduced by 34 percent from top to bottom canopy

---

TABLE 1. Influence of canopy position on characteristics of nonflowering vegetative spurs of Oregon Spur Delicious trees in Manson, Washington (after Barritt, et al., 1987).

Canopy position	Leaf characteristics/spur			Leaf efficiency[2]	Spur bud diameter (mm)
	Number	Area (cm^2)	Spur efficiency[1]		
Top	10.3	175	1.46	8.0	4.2
Middle	10.2	178	1.15	6.1	3.9
Bottom	8.8	129	0.60	4.4	3.3
Average	9.8	161	1.08	6.1	3.7
% reduction from top to bottom	−15%	−26%	−59%	-45%	−21%

[1] *Spur efficiency equals leaf dry weight (g) per spur.*
[2] *Leaf efficiency equals specific leaf weight (mg/cm^2).*

positions *(Ferree, 1983)*. It is obvious that spurs in the bottom canopy position produce less photosynthetic products, the carbohydrates needed for fruit set, fruit growth and development, than spurs in the top canopy positions.

It is interesting to note that fruiting spurs have less leaf area and lower leaf and spur efficiency than vegetative spurs *(compare Tables 1 and 2)*. Vegetative spurs use the products of photosynthesis primarily for leaf and bud development, while fruiting spurs use the products of photosynthesis to support growth of the fruit, as well as leaf and bud growth. Because fruiting spurs have a smaller and less efficient photosynthetic factory, they are less

---

TABLE 2. Influence of canopy position on fruiting spur characteristics of Oregon Spur Delicious trees in Manson, Washington, (after Barritt, et al., 1987).

| Canopy position | Leaf characteristics/spur | | | Leaf efficiency[2] | Spur bud diameter (mm) | Fruit set (%) |
	Number	Area (cm²)	Spur efficiency[1]			
Top	10.8	135	.98	7.0	3.5	61
Middle	10.9	150	.87	5.6	3.2	54
Bottom	10.1	129	.62	4.5	3.0	42
Average	10.5	138	.82	5.6	3.2	52
% reduction from top to bottom	−6%	−4%	−37%	-36%	−14%	−31%

[1] *Spur efficiency equals dry weight (g) per spur.*
[2] *Leaf efficiency equals specific leaf weight (mg/cm²).*

likely than vegetative spurs to initiate and develop a flower cluster for the next year.

Vegetative spurs in the top canopy position have greater potential to produce flower clusters and set fruit than weaker spurs in the bottom position. Fruiting spurs in the top canopy position have a greater potential to set fruit and to produce large, high quality apples than do spurs in the bottom canopy position.

SUNLIGHT AND SPUR QUALITY

Spur and leaf efficiency were substantially lower in the bottom canopy position in comparison with the top canopy position. Why do the lower parts of the tree canopy have poor quality spurs with a smaller and less efficient photosynthetic factory than spurs in other canopy positions? The obvious factor to examine is sunlight, because it is sunlight that fuels the photosynthetic factory in spur leaves.

Light interception and light distribution Light is a complicated subject, because it is not only a question of how much light a tree intercepts but also the distribution of sunlight to all parts of the canopy. The amount of sunlight intercepted by an orchard canopy has been shown to be directly related to fruit yield per acre. Sunlight which reaches the orchard floor rather than hitting the orchard canopy is wasted. Young trees which have not yet filled their space have low light interception, e.g., third-year trees at Wenatchee, Washington, intercept just 20 to 30 percent of the available sunlight.

Trees which are very large with limbs extending over the tractor row, such as the large umbrella canopies of older open-center trees, intercept a very high percentage of sunlight. However, because these canopies are so large, upper limbs shade lower limbs and outside branches shade inside branches, resulting in a poor distribution of sunlight throughout the canopy. Generally, the larger the tree canopy, the greater the problem of poor light distribution. We need to evaluate spur quality in relation to the distribution of sunlight in the canopy.

Light level and canopy position Using the same large, 17-year-old, well-trained, central leader Oregon Spur Delicious/MM 104 trees, we measured sunlight levels in the center of the canopy at three heights above soil level: 1, 2, and 3 meters (3.3, 6.5, and 10 feet). The instrument used to determine light levels measures only the light that is utilized by leaves for photosynthesis. Light is measured within the canopy, and these values are presented as a percentage of full sunlight levels measured above the tree canopy.

The average sunlight level at harvest in 1985 at the top canopy position was 48 percent of full sunlight, at the middle canopy position 23 percent, and at the bottom position 9 percent. With the same trees, light levels were measured on 10 dates throughout the 1986 growing season *(Figure 1)*. It is obvious that extremely low light levels at the middle and bottom canopy positions occurred from shortly after full bloom (FB) until harvest, a period of four months. It is generally believed that, if sunlight levels fall below 30 percent of full sunlight, serious problems occur with flower bud initiation and development, fruit set, and fruit quality. The greater the canopy thickness, the lower the light penetration into the center of the canopy.

Light level and spur quality Is there a relationship between sunlight levels in the canopy and spur quality? The answer is "yes" for some spur characteristics and "no" for others. A relationship was not found between sunlight level in the canopy and number of leaves per spur, average leaf size, or leaf area per spur.

However, with Oregon Spur Delicious, there was a relationship between sunlight levels and spur efficiency (leaf dry weight per spur) and leaf efficiency (specific leaf weight). As sunlight levels increased so did leaf and spur efficiency. A similar trend with leaf efficiency was observed with Golden Delicious in Ohio *(Ferree, 1983)*. This trend was found not only with large, pyramid-shaped, central leader trees, but also with Golden Delicious trees on a low trellis and with slender spindle trees. In summary, it can be said, that with all cultivars and growing systems and fruit growing regions, high quality spurs will be found only in

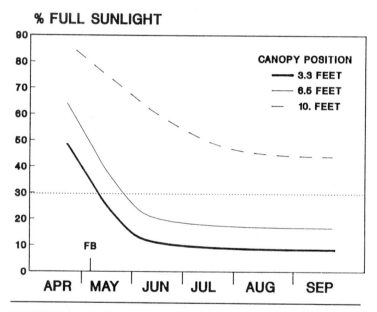

FIGURE 1. Sunlight levels in 17-year-old Oregon Spur Delicious trees at three canopy positions from before full bloom (FB) to the end of the growing season.

locations within the tree canopy with high sunlight levels.

The spur characteristics most seriously reduced in the bottom canopy position were spur efficiency and leaf efficiency. These are the same characteristics that were most seriously reduced at low sunlight levels. Therefore, with Oregon Spur Delicious, the factor most responsible for differences in spur quality from the top to bottom canopy position is sunlight level. The more the spur is exposed to light, the higher are the spur quality factors of leaf efficiency and spur efficiency that are related to the rate and size of the photosynthetic factory.

The next question that needs to be answered is whether there is a relationship between spur quality and fruit quality.

SPUR QUALITY AND FRUIT QUALITY

Fruit quality was evaluated on the same twelve, 17-year-old, central leader-trained Oregon Spur Delicious/MM 104 trees. Fruit was collected for quality evaluation at the top, middle, and bottom canopy positions, where spur quality and sunlight level were also determined. Fruit was evaluated for size, color, soluble solids, starch, and levels of nitrogen, potassium, and calcium.

Canopy position and fruit quality   Canopy position had a tremendous influence on fruit quality and maturity. Fruit at the top canopy position was larger (there was a higher percentage of fruit of size 88 and larger), had more red color, and had higher soluble solids than fruit from the bottom canopy position *(Table 3)*. A lower percentage of fruit of box size 125 and smaller was found at the top canopy position than the middle or bottom position. Fruit at the top position also had lower starch levels and lower fruit tissue levels of nitrogen, potassium, and calcium than fruit in the bottom position.

Spur characteristics and fruit quality Leaves per spur, average leaf size, or total leaf area per spur were not associated with any fruit quality traits. However, spur efficiency was correlated with fruit size and with fruit nitrogen and potassium content. The highest correlation of fruit characteristics was with leaf efficiency. As leaf efficiency increased, there were significant increases in fruit size and soluble solids, and decreases in starch content and tissue levels of nitrogen, potassium, magnesium, and calcium *(Table 3)*.

Light levels and fruit quality Large fruit size (size 88 and larger) and fruit soluble solids were positively correlated with sunlight levels. These are universal relationships, as similar correlations have been observed in Washington State with Miller Sturdeespur Delicious *(Robinson et al., 1982)* and with many other cultivars in other fruit growing regions *(Barritt, 1982)*. Small fruit size (size 125 and smaller), fruit nitrogen content, and starch level decreased with increasing sunlight levels. Red

---

TABLE 3. Influence of canopy position on sunlight level and fruit quality of Oregon Spur Delicious trees in Manson, Washington (after Barritt, et al., 1987).

Canopy position	% Full sunlight	Percent of fruit in box sizes 125 and smaller	88 and larger	Red skin color (%)	Starch rating	Soluble solids (%)	N (%)	K (%)	Ca (ppm)
Top	48	33	30	88	2.7	13.1	.15	.62	193
Middle	23	45	23	80	3.2	12.5	.20	.65	225
Bottom	9	68	6	81	3.5	12.5	.22	.68	240

68

skin color inceases with higher sunlight levels, but with the highly coloring Oregon Spur strain, the variability in color was small.

In summary, differences in spur characteristics associated with canopy position are the result of differences in light penetration to various parts of the canopy. The higher the light levels, the greater the spur quality indicators, leaf and spur efficiency. Leaf efficiency not only responds to light levels but is also correlated with rate of photosynthesis. Knowing that both spur quality and fruit quality respond in a positive way to increasing sunlight levels, maintaining adequate light penetration to all parts of the tree canopy must be a very high priority for every apple grower.

Evaluating the light situation Should growers measure leaf efficiency (specific leaf weight) to determine if light levels are too low in parts of their apple tree canopies? Should orchardists routinely make light measurements to be sure that levels are above the critical 30 percent full sunlight? Both of these measurements could show if spur quality were low, and could be used to estimate fruit size and quality. However, these are laborious procedures and require specific techniques and equipment. There is an easier way to determine if there is insufficient light to produce quality fruit. **Let the apples be light meters.**

During the final weeks before harvest, carefully observe fruit size and color. It is important to examine fruit in separate parts of the tree, particularly in the lower and inside parts of the canopy. If, in some parts of the tree, most fruit would not make Fancy grade, when fruit on the outside of the tree would be Extra Fancy, there is a light problem. If fruit is more than three box sizes smaller in some parts of the tree compared to fruit on the outside of the canopy, there is a light problem. Apples, when used as light meters, tell the story of excessive shading.

Light problems are serious problems. Light problems directly affect profitability. Orchardists are paid on the basis of fruit size, fruit color. and total production, all of which are directly influenced by sunlight levels in the tree canopy. **Light management** is achieved through proper pruning and training. Limb removal, use of limb spreaders, and reducing excessive growth in the tops of trees are established techniques to improve light penetration to all parts of the canopy *(Barritt and Rom, 1986)*. These topics, collectively termed "tree renovation," are discussed in the second part of this chapter.

Renovation pruning for light management

The true measure of an orchard system is how profitable it is and how easy it is to manage after it reaches 10 years of age. Most orchard systems can produce fruit of large size and good color during the formative training years, usually up to the tenth year. However, with older trees, pruning costs may become very high, dormant pruning may not adequately control growth, fruit size decreases, and poor fruit color occurs. These problems usually result when the guidelines for the orchard system are either misunderstood or not followed correctly. These problems cannot always be avoided with mature trees, if the variety/rootstock combination is overly vigorous for the tree spacing, or the design of the orchard system is faulty.

In the Pacific Northwest, the freestanding central leader, pyramid-shaped tree is the most commonly used orchard management system for spur-type Delicious. This system has been described in detail by Don Heinicke *(USDA Agr. Bul. 458, 1975)*. Usually, large, high quality fruit is produced on these trees dur-

70

ing the first 10 years. Some growers begin to see problems with fruit quality, usually small fruit size and poor color, by the tenth year. On the other hand, many growers do not. In recent years, the industry's problems with small fruit size and poor color are often attributed to poorly trained, central leader trees. A solution that is frequently suggested is to discard the central leader tree altogether and go back to an open-center tree. We agree that a fruit quality problem exists in many orchards but strongly disagree that open-center trees will solve the problem. The renovation of problem central leader trees is possible and practical.

What are the factors which lead to problems of poor quality, and what can be done with older central leader trees to solve the problems? To answer these questions, we must first understand the importance of light to fruit growth and fruit quality and the devastating effects of shade. When sunlight levels in a tree canopy are reduced below 30 percent of full sunlight, the situation becomes critical.

We first see poor fruit color. This may be a problem for several years before any other problems are observed. The second problem that occurs is small fruit size. By the time size is a problem, fruit color is already inadequate, so Extra Fancy fruit is not found in the shady parts of the tree. The third problem is harder to see but considerably more serious; that is poor fruit set. Poor fruit set leads directly to low production. The fourth, and most serious, concern in areas of the tree which receive less that 30 percent full sunlight, is poor flower bud initiation and development, which results in fewer flower clusters.

This trend, from poor fruit color, to small fruit size, to poor fruit set, to no flower clusters at all, occurs gradually in shaded areas over a 3- to 5-year period. It is common in trees over 12 years of age to have a major portion of the tree pass through all these stages and produce no fruit at all.

How is it possible to have these problems in central leader-trained trees? We have measured light levels from before bloom to harvest in well-trained, 4 meters (13 feet) tall, central leader trees *(Figure 1)*. At the top canopy position, 3 meters (10 feet) above the ground, sunlight levels declined gradually throughout the summer, from over 80 percent of full sunlight before bloom, to approximately 50 percent of full sunlight by July 1, and remained at that level until harvest. In the center of the tree, at 2 meters (6.5 feet) above the ground, percent of full sunlight declined from over 65 percent before bloom to 30 percent by the end of May, and remained at approximately 20 percent from June to September. At the center of the canopy, 1 meter (3.3 feet) above the ground level, percent of full sunlight levels declined rapidly until the end of May, and remained at approximately 10 percent for the rest of the season. It is disturbing to realize that in the low and mid-canopy positions, light levels were below 30 percent of full sunlight for four months of the growing season.

Studies with spur-type Red Delicious in north central Washington State showed that fruit quality traits such as size, color, and soluble solids were reduced in direct proportion to reductions in sunlight levels. It is generally not the shade from adjacent trees in the row or from adjacent rows that causes the problem, but it is the shade that a tree casts upon itself.

How do we reduce the problem of small, poorly colored fruit in older central leader trees? One obvious answer is to let more light into the tree canopy. There are four strategies to improve light distribution:

    1) Remove whole limbs;
    2) Return the tree to a pyramid shape;
    3) Reduce tree height;
    4) Spread upper and lower limbs.

Limb removal Removing whole limbs with a chain saw appears to be drastic but, in the long run, has the greatest impact on improving light penetration to all parts of the canopy. In the lower two-thirds of the canopy, any limb that is directly over another and less than 1 meter (3 feet) above it, is a candidate for removal. Limbs are removed to provide light windows into the center of the canopy.

In the top third of the tree, strongly growing branches that are greater than two-thirds the diameter of the central leader at the point of attachment should be removed completely. If branches are not removed, they become strongly upright and vegetative, creating a larger canopy which shades lower limbs.

Pyramid shape It is imperative that the canopy retain the Christmas tree or pyramid shape. Those limbs that are retained must be stubbed (shortened) back into older wood to a weak side shoot or spur. This is required for limbs at all positions in the canopy if they extend beyond the outline of the pyramid. Heading cuts into one-year-old wood are not appropriate, as they only stimulate (invigorate) shoot growth in the region of the cut.

Tree height The taller the tree, the greater the problem of poor light distribution in the lower canopy. Reduced tree height is accomplished by removal of the top of the central leader by cutting into older wood, often 3- or 4-year-old wood. Tree height should not be greater than 12 feet for central leader spur Delicious at a row spacing of 18 feet (rule: maximum height = two-thirds row spacing).

Spreading Upright limbs tend to be vigorous and always shade the inner canopy. Permanent limbs should not be greater than 45 degrees above the horizontal. Even older limbs on 10-year-old trees can be spread to 45 degrees with long spreaders. This opens up the center of the tree canopy to sunlight. In the top one-third of the tree, limbs can be spread to the horizontal. This results in less extension growth, because horizontal limbs are less vigorous and fruit heavily.

Some trees are easier to maintain and renovate after they reach 10 years of age than others. There is no doubt that, on a given site, trees on seedling rootstock are more difficult to renovate and to maintain in their proper pyramid shape than trees on clonal rootstock such as M 2, M 4, M 7, MM 106, and MM 111. This is because trees on seedling are more vigorous, requiring more wood to be removed, but, at the same time, responding to heavy cuts with extensive sucker growth. It is important to watch nitrogen fertilizer levels and perhaps eliminate a fall application before renovation and a spring application after renovation.

When renovation is required, should it be done at one time? Generally, yes. The best approach to prevent the problem is to remove limbs gradually during the tree's developmental years, from ages 7 to 10. However, if this has not been done and a serious problem has occurred, as it almost always will if limb removal is not practiced, it is best to remove at one time the limbs that are causing the shade problem. To postpone the removal of some limbs will only delay the time to recovery and elimination of the problem.

Watch for signs of improvement in your trees, but don't expect a turnaround in the number and vigor of flower clusters in the lower portion of the tree in the first year. It takes more than one year for a spur to rejuvenate. The first year a spur is exposed to more light, the leaf number will not increase significantly. However, the bud on the spur will be stronger at the end of the first growing season, because the spur will be stronger, have greater leaf number, and leaf area, and will probably develop a flower bud. Only by the third year will improvement in flower cluster number be observed.

Improvement in fruit color will occur the summer after renovation. However, individual fruit size will not improve much the first year. Fruit size will improve significantly the second year after renovation, because the spurs are stronger with greater leaf area, and because the renovation pruning is also a thinning technique, with fewer but larger fruits being retained. In the third year after renovation pruning, fruit size had improved dramatically in the middle and bottom canopy positions *(Table 4)*. With renovation pruning, fruit in the bottom canopy position increased from 21 percent size 88 and larger to 45 percent size 88 and larger. There was a decrease in the percentage of small fruit, box size 125 and smaller, from 39 percent for standard pruning to 20 percent for renovation pruning at the bottom canopy position.

Improvement in spur growth can be seen when old spur systems are exposed to light. Rather than the usual 1.25 centimeters (half-inch) of growth each year, short shoots 15 centimeters (6 inches) or larger will occur on older spurs. This increase in leaf number and area on the spur makes the spur stronger and more

TABLE 4. The effect of renovation pruning and tree canopy position on the percentage of fruit of box size 88 and larger, 100 to 113, and 125 and smaller. These results were obtained the third year after heavy renovation pruning.

Canopy position	88 and larger		100 to 113		125 and smaller	
	standard pruning	renovation pruning	standard pruning	renovation pruning	standard pruning	renovation pruning
Top*	61	64	28	27	12	9
Middle	40	51	41	38	19	12
Bottom	21	45	40	36	39	20

*Top is 10' above ground level, middle is 6.5' above ground, and bottom is 3.3' above ground.

likely to flower, set fruit, and produce large fruit in subsequent years.

The drastic heavy pruning cuts of renovation may not be required on all central leader-trained spur Delicious trees. In fact, with careful tree training, drastic renovation should not be required at all. The critical times in light management are from years 1 to 5, and 7 to 9. Growers almost always do an excellent job of limb removal and positioning during the 1- to 5-year stage. However, many growers, seeing fruit on the 7- to 9-year-old trees, are reluctant to remove a limb or two or stub back limbs to retain the pyramid shape. It is essential that light penetrate to all parts of the tree at the 7- to 9-year stage, if growers are to avoid the fruit quality and production declines after year 10. The best preventive action is taken in years 7 to 9. Most growers say they know when to remove an extra shading limb, but, unfortunately, few growers actually do it during the critical 7- to 9-year stage and, therefore, develop problems that can only be solved by the heavy cuts of renovation. To make the critical pruning cuts at the right time requires a complete understanding of the devastating effects of shade on fruit production and fruit quality.

We gratefully acknowledge the cooperation of the Wells and Wade Fruit Company, the technical assistance of Bonnie Schonberg and Marc Dilley, and the financial support of the Washington Tree Fruit Research Commission.

Additional reading

Barritt, B.H. 1982. Prosper in the '80's by letting your trees see the light. Proc. Wash. State Hort. Assoc. 78:10-16.

Barritt, B.H. and C.R. Rom. 1987. Management of apple

fruiting spurs for fruit quality and profitability. Parts 3 and 4. *Good Fruit Grower* 38(21):58, 59, 91.

Barritt, B.H., C.R. Rom, and S.R. Drake. 1987. Management of apple fruiting spurs for fruit quality and profitability. Part 5. Spur quality and fruit quality. *Good Fruit Grower* 38(21):102.

Barritt, B.H., C.R. Rom, K.R. Guelich, S.R. Drake, and M.A. Dilley. 1987. Canopy position and light effects on spur, leaf, and fruit characteristics of Delicious apple. *HortScience* 22:402-405.

Ferree, D.C. 1983. Managing light in the high density orchard. Proc. Wash. State Hort. Assoc. 79:129-133.

Heinicke, D.R. 1975. High-density apple orchards – planning, training, and pruning. USDA Handbook 458.

Robinson, T., E.J. Seeley, and B.H. Barritt. 1982. Light intensity, spur age effects on fruit quality. *Good Fruit Grower* 33(6):32, 33, 36.

Rom, C.R. 1985. How spur quality influences fruit size. Proc. Wash. State Hort. Assoc. 81:109-118.

Rom, C.R. and B.H. Barritt. 1987. Management of apple fruiting spurs for fruit quality and profitability. Parts 1 and 2. *Good Fruit Grower* 38(21):14, 16-18, 20-23, 58.

5 DECIDING ON A HIGH DENSITY ORCHARD SYSTEM

By Bruce H. Barritt

WHEN PLANNING A NEW ORCHARD, THE FOLLOWING FACTORS MUST be considered: the variety, rootstock, tree density, tree arrangement (single versus multiple rows), tree shape, tree pruning and training, tree support system, and management skill. When all of these components are brought together into an organized plan, it is termed an "orchard system." For example, the freestanding central leader tree, widely grown in Washington State for the past 20 years, is an orchard system with the following components: medium to vigorous rootstock, tree density of 250 to 400 trees per acre, arranged in single rows, without tree support, and pruned and trained to a pyramid shape. The guidelines for this orchard system were developed by Don Heinicke and described in 1975 in USDA Agricultural Handbook 458. Other orchard systems include the French vertical axis, the Dutch slender spindle, the palmette, and the Tatura, Lincoln, and Ebro trellises.

Goals of an orchard system

There must be good reason for changing to a new orchard system. The important reason a new orchard system is chosen is because it either reduces or eliminates the major problem with an older orchard system. For example, with many growers in the Pacific Northwest, the freestanding central leader system used for the past 20 years has two problems. First, the large trees have a high labor cost for thinning, pruning, and harvesting. Second, the trees may take 4 to 6 years to come into bearing and, therefore, are slow at paying for the costs of establishment.

French growers with similar goals changed to the vertical axis system *(Lespinasse, 1980)*. The Dutch apple industry had similar reasons for changing, along with the need to change vari-

80

eties, and adopted the high density slender spindle system *(Wertheim, 1985)*. A high density system is recommended in New York State to simplify management, reduce production and harvest costs, and improve fruit quality *(Norton, 1988)*. For Pacific Northwest growers with these problems, a new orchard system with smaller trees may reduce labor costs, and one that comes into bearing sooner may reduce the interest expense during the development period of the orchard.

Another example of a goal would be to reduce the labor cost of harvesting by using picking aids or mechanical harvesting. Picking aids work best with relatively narrow-walled hedgerows such as the palmette, while the Tatura trellis and Lincoln canopy systems were developed specifically for mechanical harvesting. Picking aids are used to a limited extent in some fruit districts, but mechanical harvesting of apples for fresh market is not a commercial reality today and may not be for many years.

If the goal of an orchardist is to plant a new variety that may return high prices, he will want early production. He will select a new orchard system that uses dwarfing rootstocks that allow him to plant at a high tree density. The higher the tree density, the higher the early yield. He will also plant a precocious rootstock to ensure that the tree comes into bearing early. To meet these goals, the M 26, Mark, and M 9 rootstocks would be considered. Tree densities of 800 to 1,200 trees per acre would be appropriate.

To repeat, a new orchard system will be chosen that reduces or eliminates the problems encountered with an established orchard system. The problems may be high labor costs, lack of early production, low production, poor fruit quality, or the wrong variety. The goal of a new orchard system is to eliminate these factors which reduce profitability of the older system. In the end, profitability, the ultimate goal, equates to economic considerations such as price per pound of fruit, production level, and orchard establishment costs. These economic factors are discussed by G. Geldart in chapter eight.

The orchard system puzzle

As we have seen, an orchard system is an integration of factors resulting in a specific tree density, tree size, and tree form. Selecting the right components for a new orchard system can be similar to completing a jigsaw puzzle. The many components of an orchard system must fit together, like pieces of a puzzle, to make a complete and successful new orchard. The pieces of the orchard system puzzle are orchard site, variety, rootstock, spacing, tree training, support, and management skill *(Figure 1)*. The components must all be considered before trees are planted and, by wise growers, before trees are ordered. These puzzle pieces must be considered as interacting pieces, because, if any one piece of the puzzle is missing or does not fit with the others, the orchard system will not be successful.

Factors to consider

Site The orchard site will have a greater influence on long-term profitability than any other factor. Severe mid winter freezes can kill or severely and permanently damage trees. For most fruit areas, test winters occur only on an irregular basis. However, in the coldest districts, injury may occur every year, and these areas should not be planted to any orchard system. Spring frosts are a more common problem that can reduce or eliminate a crop. Sites with a severe spring frost problem every year should not be planted to any orchard system. If spring frosts occur some years, measures can be taken to reduce

82

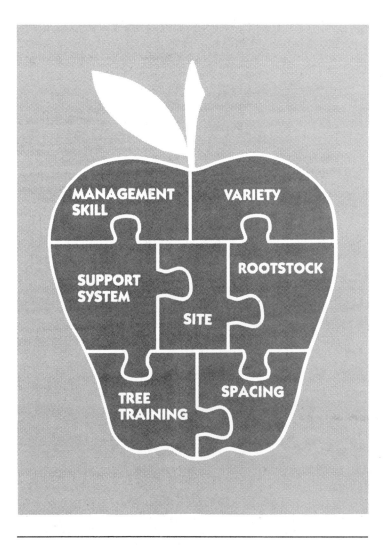

FIGURE 1. The orchard system puzzle.

the problem, e.g., wind machines or sprinklers. New orchard systems with small trees should not be planted in sites with spring frost problems unless methods to reduce the problem are incorporated into the design of the new orchard.

In high density orchards with relatively small trees, if an early crop is lost due to spring frost, the profitability of the orchard is affected, not only for the year of the crop loss, but also for future years. Because of the loss of an early crop, the interest expense increases considerably, delaying the time to the break-even point. In addition, the loss of a crop results in increased growth, which requires extra expense in pruning and training to maintain the trees in their allotted space.

Another factor associated with orchard site is the need for irrigation. In central Washington, irrigation is an absolute requirement. The extent to which an orchardist has control of irrigation practices can influence tree growth and productivity. With dwarfing rootstocks, root growth is limited, and, consequently, they extract water from a small soil volume. This means more frequent irrigation is required.

Wind is an aspect of site that influences tree growth. Unsupported trees cannot be trained properly in windy sites. Trees in high density orchards, which are supported with individual posts or a trellis, generally can be trained easily and crop well in relatively windy sites. At very windy sites, windbreaks should be established.

Rootstock Tree size and, therefore, tree density, are determined by two pieces of the orchard system puzzle, rootstock and variety. Rootstock is by far the most important factor, and the factor that should be considered first. It is not possible to establish high density orchards of non-spur cultivars on rootstocks equal to, or with more vigor than, M 7. For example, MM 106, MM 111, M 4, M 2, or seedling are not suitable, because these trees become too large. The rootstocks of choice for high density plantings are M 26 and M 9, and possibly for trial, the new rootstock Mark. However, with less vigorous spur-type strains of Delicious, M 7 is an appropriate rootstock for planting orchards at approximately 500 trees per acre.

Variety The major reason to change varieties is based on the low returns growers receive for the Delicious variety, particularly in comparison with returns from newer varieties such as Granny Smith and Gala. Growth and fruiting habit of varieties influence the decision about rootstock, tree density, tree training, and support system. Spur-type strains of Red Delicious are a distinct group and must be considered separately from all non-spur varieties and from the relatively vigorous spur-type strains of Rome, McIntosh, Golden Delicious, and Granny Smith.

Spur-type strains of Delicious have a compact growth habit. This means that they will produce a considerably smaller tree than a non-spur strain when grown on the same rootstock. This reduced vigor is due to fewer lateral shoots (more spurs instead) and shorter shoot growth. Spur-type strains on weak sites (i.e., with replant problems), or on weak rootstocks, often fail to produce enough shoot growth to produce large, high quality fruit. The term "runt out" is used to describe these trees that fail to grow, and overcrop with small fruit. To avoid this problem, dwarfing rootstocks such as M 9, Mark, and M 26 should generally be avoided for spur-type Delicious. An exception might be M 26 on a heavier soil with good water-holding capacity and with an irrigation system that can supply water frequently. Orchard systems for spur-type Delicious have been discussed by Peterson (1989).

On the other hand, on non-spur (standard) growth habit varieties, growth will be excessive with vigorous rootstocks (seedling, MM 111, M 2, M 4, and MM 106). For example, non-spur growth cultivars like Gala on M 7 will be a much larger tree than a spur-type Delicious on M 7 and would, therefore, need to be planted at a lower tree density. If non-spur cultivars are to be planted at high densities, they must be planted on dwarfing rootstocks, rootstocks producing a tree at least as small as M 26 and perhaps smaller. As pieces of the orchard system puzzle, the variety and its growth habit, along with the vigor of the rootstock, must fit together to achieve a manageable orchard.

As an example, a grower has selected a vigorous non-spur cultivar, Gala, as the variety he wants to grow, and he wants to plant a high density orchard of over 600 trees per acre. He is able to obtain trees of Gala on M 7. Unfortunately, two pieces of the puzzle, the rootstock and spacing, do not fit together, as M 7 is too vigorous a rootstock with most soils for a non-spur variety planted at 600 trees per acre.

As a second example, a grower wants to plant spur-type Delicious, a weak-growing cultivar, at 600 trees per acre. For this high density planting, he has obtained trees on M 9 rootstock. The two pieces of the puzzle that do not fit together are the variety and the rootstock. Even though M 9 will produce a small tree, allowing the grower to plant at least 600 trees per acre, M 9 with spur Delicious will produce a tree that is too weak and will not grow sufficiently (it will runt out) to achieve high production and high fruit quality.

Spacing Once the variety and rootstock are chosen, the possible spacings are limited. In single-row plantings, tree spacing for standard cultivars on M 26 is 5 to 7 feet in the row and 13 to 15 feet between rows, giving tree densities of 415 to 670 trees per acre. For M 9 and Mark, in-row spacing of 4 to 6 feet and between-row spacing of 12 to 14 feet will provide tree densities of 519 to 908 trees per acre.

For spur-type Delicious, dwarfing rootstocks like M 26 are

generally too weak in Washington State and are not recommended. This means that truly high density orchards with over 600 trees per acre of spur-type Delicious are probably not feasible on most sites *(Peterson, 1989)*. Spur-type Delicious on M 7 as a freestanding tree can be planted 6 to 8 feet apart in rows 14 to 17 feet apart, giving tree densities of 320 to 519 trees per acre.

If Delicious is the variety of choice, and a truly high density orchard of 600 to 1,000 trees per acre is desired, a non-spur strain of Delicious on M 26, M 9, or Mark at spacings given above for non-spur varieties would be a realistic possibility. It is not possible to give exact spacings, so ranges are provided, allowing for differences in 1) site and soil, 2) vigor of the variety, e.g., Jonagold is more vigorous than Empire, and 3) training system chosen, e.g., slender spindle trees are smaller than vertical axis trees.

After the selection of a dwarfing rootstock, it is tree training and pruning that are the primary ways trees can be kept within their allotted space. Although it is generally believed that M 9 trees are always small, a non-spur variety on M 9 can grow to 8 feet wide and 10 feet tall. Maintaining the tree in a small space is much easier with rootstocks such as M 9, Mark, and M 26, than with more vigorous rootstocks. However, the keys to accomplishing and maintaining small tree size are:

1) the support systems;
2) the training systems; and
3) the management skills.

These are the three remaining pieces of the orchard system puzzle.

Support systems   Along with the decision to plant a high density orchard that has more than 500 trees per acre, goes the decision to support the trees. No matter what training system is used, with rootstocks M 26, M 9, and Mark, the central leader must be supported. These rootstocks are so precocious and set such heavy crops that the central leader cannot be maintained in a vertical position (or at a 60-degree angle in a "V" trellis) without support. Fruit can be allowed to set on a central leader that is supported. However, if fruit is allowed to set on an unsupported central leader, it will bend away from the vertical. This eliminates the possibility of using a central leader training system such as the slender spindle or vertical axis. Therefore, a support system is primarily a tree-training tool. A second, but also critical, reason for support is to prevent a heavily cropping tree from falling over. Planting a high density orchard without supporting the trees would be an extremely serious mistake. Tree support is not an option – it is a requirement.

The method of tree support is less important than the absolute need for support. It makes little difference if a tree is supported by 1) an individual pole per tree, 2) a thin bamboo or wood pole or nylon string attached to a horizontal trellis wire, 3) a 3- to 4-wire trellis, or 4) a multi-wire vee-shaped trellis. A major consideration in choosing a particular method of support is the cost of materials and labor. The critical factor is not the kind of support but that the tree be supported. Construction details for trellises are discussed by Bert van Dalfsen in chapter seven and in the publication "How to build orchard and vineyard trellises."

Tree training   There are several ways to train supported trees in a high density orchard *(Barritt, 1984)*. Two possibilities are the slender spindle *(Wertheim, 1968; 1981; 1985)* and the vertical axis *(Lespinasse, 1980; 1981)*. With slender spindle trees, the central leader is pruned away each year, and a competing side shoot is trained up the post as the new leader. This gives the central leader a zigzag appearance. Modifications to this approach involving bending and heading the central leader are also possible. Slender spindle trees are usually less than 7 feet tall. In contrast, with the vertical axis system, the central leader is not pruned away. The vertical axis tree is, therefore, a taller tree than the slender spindle.

With both systems there is a lower tier of permanent scaffold limbs. To prevent these permanent limbs from becoming too long and extending into the next tree, they are pruned back into older wood to a weak side shoot. Branches in the upper two-thirds of both slender spindle and vertical axis trees are completely removed, usually after one or two fruiting years, when they extend beyond the narrow tree form. No heading pruning cuts into one-year branches are made with slender spindle or vertical axis systems. High density training systems are discussed in greater detail by Kathleen Williams in chapter six.

Management skill   The last piece of the orchard system puzzle is management skill. If an orchardist has the desire to change to a high density system and has made a commitment to do so, he has accepted the idea that some new skills will be required. To ensure good growth on old orchard sites, he will need to address potential replant problems. He will need to refine his irrigation system for dwarfing rootstocks with limited root distribution. He will need to learn how to build a support system for weak trees. He will need to learn to use new pruning and training techniques to balance growth and fruiting. Information on these subjects is now available.

The quickest way to develop new skills is to practice them. It is prudent to start in a small way with a trial planting of a new high density system. Try a single row of a new system a year or two before planting a new orchard block. The learning experience will be invaluable and will eliminate many costly errors when it comes time to plant a new orchard block. A progressive industry is an industry that is continually learning new management skills.

Orchard systems trials

In 1985, at the Smith Tract orchard of the Tree Fruit Research and Extension Center, Wenatchee, Washington, trials of Granny Smith and Golden Delicious were established with three training systems: freestanding central leader trees at 360 trees per acre, vertical axis trees at 514 trees per acre, and slender spindle trees at 675 trees per acre *(Table 1)*. Rootstocks M 26 EMLA, M 9 EMLA, and Mark were used. "EMLA" is an abbreviation for East Malling-Long Ashton and refers to the Malling series of rootstocks which are free of known viruses.

In the third year, with both Granny Smith and Golden Delicious, the greatest production occurred for the slender spindle and vertical axis systems with the M 9 EMLA rootstock *(Table 1)*. Fourth-year production for Granny Smith with slender spindle and vertical axis systems *(Figure 2)* varied from 459 to 679 boxes per acre with M 9 EMLA, Mark, and M 26 EMLA rootstocks. Fourth-year production for Golden Delicious with slender spindle and vertical axis systems varied from 709 to 893 boxes per acre with rootstocks M 9 EMLA, Mark, and M 26 EMLA. Lowest production, with both Granny Smith and Golden Delicious, in both the third and fourth years, occurred with the freestanding central leader system.

In the third year, production generally increased with an increase in tree density, e.g., slender spindle trees had higher production per acre than vertical axis trees on the same rootstock. However, in the fourth year, vertical axis trees at 514 trees per acre reached a similar level of production per acre as slender spindle trees at 675 trees per acre, because the vertical axis trees had greater production per tree.

In a second Golden Delicious trial planted in 1985 at the Columbia View orchard of the Tree Fruit Research and Extension Center *(Table 2)*, production trends were very similar to

90

TABLE 1. Influence of orchard training system and rootstock on fruit production from Granny Smith and Golden Delicious trees planted in 1985 at the Tree Fruit Research and Extension Center Smith Tract orchard near Wenatchee, Washington.

Orchard system[2]	Rootstock	Trees /acre	Boxes/acre[1] 1987	Boxes/acre[1] 1988	Boxes/tree[1] 1987	Boxes/tree[1] 1988
GRANNY SMITH						
Central leader	Mark	360	187	315	.5	.9
	EMLA 26	360	172	229	.5	.6
Vertical axis	EMLA 9	514	395	677	.8	1.3
	Mark	514	325	595	.6	1.2
	EMLA 26	514	177	459	.3	.9
Slender spindle	EMLA 9	675	577	679	.9	1.0
	EMLA 26	675	304	564	.4	.8
GOLDEN DELICIOUS						
Central leader	Mark	360	148	372	.4	1.0
	EMLA 26	360	180	293	.5	.8
Vertical axis	EMLA 26	514	251	855	.5	1.7
Slender spindle	EMLA 9	675	439	893	.7	1.3
	Mark	675	420	709	.6	1.1
	EMLA 26	675	351	875	.5	1.3

[1]*36-pound loose boxes.*
[2]*Slender spindle and vertical axis trees are supported, central leader trees are freestanding.*

those reported above. Slender spindle trees on M 9 EMLA had the greatest production in the third year. In the fourth year, slender spindle trees on M 9 EMLA and vertical axis trees on M 9 EMLA, M 26 EMLA, and Mark all had similar yields per acre. Freestanding central leader trees consistently had the lowest production per acre.

In 1987, an orchard systems trial was established at the Tree Fruit Research and Extension Center, Wenatchee, with slender

---

TABLE 2. Influence of orchard training system and rootstock on fruit production from Golden Delicious trees planted in 1985 at the Tree Fruit Research and Extension Center Columbia View orchard near Wenatchee, Washington.

Orchard system[2]	Rootstock	Trees /acre	Boxes/acre[1] 1987	Boxes/acre[1] 1988	Boxes/tree[1] 1987	Boxes/tree[1] 1988
GOLDEN DELICIOUS						
Central leader	Mark	476	154	238	.3	.5
	EMLA 26	476	163	253	.3	.5
Vertical axis	EMLA 9	635	298	586	.5	.9
	Mark	544	264	561	.5	1.0
	EMLA 26	544	294	584	.5	1.1
Slender spindle	EMLA 9	762	400	559	.5	.7
	EMLA 26	762	204	234	.3	.3

[1] *36-pound loose boxes.*
[2] *Slender spindle and vertical axis trees are supported, central leader trees are freestanding.*

spindle trees on M 9 EMLA and Budagovsky 9 (Bud 9), vertical axis trees on M 26 EMLA and M 7 EMLA, and freestanding central leader trees on M 26 EMLA and M 7 EMLA *(Table 3)*. Four cultivars were used in the trial: Imperial Gala, Nicobel Jonagold, Criterion, and Redchief Mercier Delicious. Well-feathered trees were planted, which resulted in significant second-year yields.

Highest second-year production per acre occurred on

TABLE 3. Influence of orchard system and rootstock on second-year fruit production from a trial planted in 1987 at the Tree Fruit Research and Extension Center, Wenatchee, Washington.

Orchard system[2]	Rootstock	Trees /acre	1988 production (boxes/acre)[1]	
			Gala	4-variety average[3]
Central leader	EMLA 26	324	21	10
	EMLA 7	324	3	1
Vertical axis	EMLA 26	514	49	36
	EMLA 7	514	10	5
Slender spindle	EMLA 9	772	178	117
	Bud 9[4]	772	118	87

[1] *36-pound loose boxes.*
[2] *Slender spindle and vertical axis trees are supported, central leader trees are freestanding.*
[3] *Average of varieties Imperial Gala, Nicobel Jonagold, Criterion, and Redchief Mercier Delicious.*
[4] *Budagovsky 9, a dwarf, collar rot resistant, and winter hardy Russian rootstock.*

slender spindle trees with M 9 EMLA and Bud 9 rootstocks. With both M 26 EMLA and M 7 EMLA rootstocks, the vertical axis trees at 514 trees per acre had higher production per acre than central leader trees at 324 trees per acre. Trees on M 26 EMLA rootstock had greater second-year production than trees on M 7 EMLA rootstock. Of the four varieties in the trial, Gala had significantly higher production than the other three.

Results from high density apple trials in Washington State demonstrate that it is possible to obtain high early yields similar to those reported in Europe. Adapting the European concepts of high density orchards to the climate, soils, and varieties of central Washington State will be a challenge that will require some modifications of the introduced systems. Growers must appreciate the complexities of high density orchard systems and must thoroughly study the individual factors, for example, the rootstock and tree spacing, to develop a successful orchard. Not only must all the factors be considered, but the factors must fit together, like the pieces of a puzzle.

In summary, to understand the concepts of high density orchards, the following "Rules of High Density" must be accepted.

Rules of high density

1) High density means more than 500 trees per acre.
2) Only rootstocks M 26 size and smaller are suitable for non-spur varieties.
3) High tree density gives high early production.
4) Feathered trees produce high early yields.
5) Pruning delays early cropping.
6) Tree support is a requirement, not an option.

To survive, orchardists in the Washington State apple industry need to accept the challenge and change to high density orchard systems.

The technical assistance of Marc Dilley, Bonnie Schonberg, and Gene Fairchild is gratefully acknowledged. Funding was provided by Washington State University and the Washington Tree Fruit Research Commission.

Additional reading

Anon. 1982. How to build orchard and vineyard trellises. United States Steel Corp., Pittsburgh. 48 pp.

Barritt, B.H. 1984. Central leader training systems for apple. *Good Fruit Grower* 35(21):56-61.

Barritt, B.H. 1988. Orchard system decision depends on site, variety, and rootstock. *Good Fruit Grower* 39(3):16-19.

Barritt, B.H. 1988. Vertical axis training seen as an alternative for apples. *Good Fruit Grower* 39(3):24-26.

Granger, R.L. 1988. Modifications in the French vertical axis system of apple trees. *Compact Fruit Tree* 21:20-23.

Heinicke, D.R. 1975. High-density apple orchards – planning, training, and pruning. USDA Agr. Handbook 458. 34 pp.

Lespinasse, J.-M. 1980. La conduite du pommier, l'axe vertical la renovation des vergers 2[e] partie. Centre Technique Interprofessional des Fruits et Legumes, Paris. 120 pp.

Lespinasse, J.-M. 1981. Apple tree management in flat, vertical axis, and palmette forms, by cultivar fruiting type. Experiments with other species: plum, peach, pear, cherry. Perspectives de l'horticulture. Arbres fruitiers et petits fruits. *Colloques Scientifiques.* No. 15. Montreal, Canada. 103-130.

Maillard, A. and P. Herman. 1988. Development and management of trees in our version of the vertical axe system in Castang. *Compact Fruit Tree* 21:23-35.

Norton, R.L. 1988. The case for high density multiple row planting systems. *Good Fruit Grower* 39(18):22-24.

Peterson, B. 1989. Orchard systems for spur Delicious. *Good Fruit Grower* 40(3):4-9.

Robinson, T. and A.N. Lakso. 1988. Performance of an apple planting system trial. *Compact Fruit Tree* 21:36-40.

Rice, M. 1988. Applying the limb renewal system to our operation. *Compact Fruit Tree* 21:42-44.

Stebbins, R. 1987. The dwarf apple fruiting wall. Oregon State Univ. Special Rpt. 802. 6 pp.

Stebbins, R. 1989. Rootstock and variety affect tree efficiency. *Good Fruit Grower* 40(1):18-19.

Tukey, L.D. 1988. Experiences with the French axe. *Compact Fruit Tree* 21:16-19.

Wertheim, S.J. 1968. The training of the slender spindle. Proefstation voor de Fruitteelt, Wilhelminadorp, Pub. No. 7. 37 pp.

Wertheim, S.J. 1981. Spacing and training of slender spindle-type trees. Perspectives de l'horticulture. Arbres fruitiers et petits fruits. *Colloques Scientifiques.* No 15. Montreal, Canada. 133-167.

Wertheim, S.J. 1985. New developments in Dutch apple production. *Compact Fruit Tree* 18:1-12.

6 COMPARISON OF SLENDER SPINDLE AND VERTICAL AXIS

By Kathleen M. Williams

As the Pacific Northwest tree fruit industry moves into the 21st Century, there will be an increasing emphasis on improving orchard labor efficiency and fruit quality, as well as promoting early production. Labor for pruning and harvesting operations is, and will continue to be, the most expensive aspect of producing fruit. Improved labor efficiency depends on improved orchard design.

Large trees of the Pacific Northwest (PNW) central leader system pose significant problems in terms of orchard labor efficiency and fruit quality. We, as an industry, are looking to other orchard systems, primarily from western Europe, to improve our orchard efficiency.

Two promising systems, the slender spindle from the Netherlands and the vertical axis from France, are currently under test in Washington State. Both of these systems use a central leader tree with a supporting framework of laterals. However, there are significant differences in pruning and training techniques for producing trees in either of these orchard systems in comparison with the PNW central leader system.

▌ Slender
▌ spindle
▌ system

The slender spindle orchard system was developed in the Netherlands in the mid 1960's and has been refined throughout the past 20 years. The system was developed to design trees that could optimize light interception and distribution throughout the canopy under the low-light conditions in the Netherlands.

Furthermore, the trees had to be physically easy to train, prune, and maintain, because the Dutch labor supply depends on local people. The trees also had to come into production early to repay the high initial capital expenditure required and allow

98

growers the option to replant their orchards to newer, more profitable cultivars. The slender spindle and vertical axis systems were developed and continue to be utilized primarily in the management of non-spur cultivars such as Golden Delicious.

The slender spindle tree is a pyramid-shaped tree that is always planted on a dwarfing rootstock, mainly M 9. Trees are always supported with either a post or stake. Tree height is maintained at 6 to 7 feet, and tree spread is generally restricted to 3 to 3.5 feet in a single-row design. Tree density is 1,000 trees or more per acre, depending on the tree spacing. *(See Table 1)*.

TRAINING THE SLENDER SPINDLE TREE

Year 1 – at planting: A branched or "feathered" nursery tree is always preferable to a non-branched "whip" as planting stock, because production will occur at least one year earlier.

The branched tree is headed 10 to 15 inches above the highest retained branch. If there are upright branches present which cannot be trained to a more horizontal angle, they are removed. Branches below 18 inches above the soil line are removed, because they will interfere with herbicide applications, and the fruit will be too low for convenient and clean harvest. If a whip is planted, it is headed 33 to 39 inches above the soil line.

Year 1 – summer (first leaf): Vigorous branches are tied or weighted down to the horizontal with non-spur varieties. For spur types, a less extreme horizontal angle is appropriate, e.g., 45 to 60 degrees. It is important with spur types not to train weak branches to a horizontal angle; the branches will be devigorated by fruiting and will eventually "runt out."

The optimum time for limb positioning, if tying or weigh-

TABLE 1. Comparison of central leader training systems for non-spur apple cultivars (after Barritt, 1984).

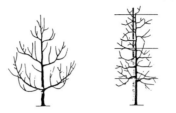

	PNW Head & Spread	Vertical Axis	Slender Spindle
Tree height	10-15 feet	10-14 feet	7-8 feet
Tree spread at base	7-10 feet	4-6 feet	4-6 feet
Spacing of single rows	16-20 feet	13-16 feet	10-12 feet
Tree density	220-400 trees/acre	450-800 trees/acre	700-1,100 trees/acre
Rootstocks	M 26, M 7, MM 106, MM 111, seedling	M 9, M 26, M 7	M 9, Mark
Tree support	None	Pole & wires	Post or stake
At planting head the tree	Yes	Yes	Yes
Select 3 to 5 permanent lower scaffold limbs	Yes	Yes	Yes
Head central leader in dormant season	Yes	No	No
Pruning of central leader after year one	Head into 1-year-old wood. To maintain height, cut to lateral.	No heading. To maintain height, cut to replacement leader.	Head to competing lateral on older wood.
Remove central leader to weaker side shoot in each dormant season	Yes	No	No
Head scaffolds in dormant season	Yes	No	No
Spread or tie down branches	Yes, to 45° from vertical	Yes	Yes, to the horizontal
Control limb length by cutting back into older wood	Yes	Yes	Yes, lower tier
Control limb length by removal to trunk	No	Yes, upper limbs, leaving a stub.	Yes, upper limbs, leaving a stub.

100

ing down, is mid July to mid August. However, earlier improvement of branch angles with young shoots three to six inches in length can be achieved with clothespins or toothpicks. Care must be taken to keep the terminal ends of the branches at a horizontal or slightly vertical angle; they should not be allowed to bend down, as this can cause excessive vigor in the lower portions of the branch. On spur types, extreme downward bending can be too devigorating.

The first summer is when most of the pruning is conducted on the young slender spindle tree. Vigorous upright branches, which compete with the leader, are completely eliminated. Lateral branches with narrow angles are removed. The desirable wood to leave is weak, horizontal branches.

Year 2 – dormant pruning (1st dormant season following planting): If summer training and pruning operations were conducted during the first growing season, very little dormant pruning is required. However, if vigorous branches or upright growth were not removed, now is the time to do this operation. Vigorous growth should not be allowed to remain for 2 seasons; the growth and vigor of the leader and other lateral branches will be unbalanced.

The central leader is removed by heading into 2-year-old wood to a competing lateral. An alternative method of central leader vigor control is to bend over the central leader the previous summer, then return the leader to the other side of the supporting post the following spring (May or June). In this method, no heading cuts are made during the second winter. *(See Figure 1)*. The leader of a non-spur variety should not be headed into 1-year-old wood.

The scaffold branches for the lower permanent tier are selected; there are generally 3 to 5 permanent lower branches. Scaffold branches are **never** headed into 1-year-old wood, as this

FIGURE 1. Slender spindle tree (Gala on Mark) after dormant pruning, year 2. Note that the central leader was not headed; rather, it was bent over the previous summer and will be brought back to the other side of the post the following spring. Notice that the scaffold branches have been "singled" and that upright growth was removed from the scaffolds.

type of pruning cut is too invigorating. Also, heading cuts into 1-year-old wood delay fruiting.

Year 2 – summer training and pruning: As in year 1, limb positioning of lateral branches should be continued and undesirable growth removed. Proper limb positioning is critical for flower bud initiation and development. Growth which competes with the leader or is excessively vigorous should not be allowed to develop during the growing season. Timing and techniques for training and pruning are the same as those for year 1 summer.

Year 3: The tree should be in commercial production by year 3 (third leaf), if a branched nursery tree was planted. Dormant and summer pruning utilize the same techniques as employed in the first and second growing seasons. However, lower scaffolds will need to be shortened with the use of stubbing cuts into 2-year-old wood. The leader will continue to be pruned to a replacement lateral or tied over as in previous years.

Continued pruning of the central leader to a competing lateral, which is then trained upwards, results in a central leader with a zigzag shape. This zigzag configuration helps to reduce excessive growth in the top of the tree as the tree matures.

Year 4: By the fourth leaf, maintenance pruning is conducted. There are three major steps to remember:

1) Renew upper scaffolds: after a branch has fruited, it is generally removed by pruning it off completely and leaving a short stub. *(See Figure 2a).*

2) Shorten lower scaffolds: head to a weak lateral on older wood. This is used to restrict the tree to its allotted space. *(See Figure 2b).*

3) Control central leader growth: use either replacement

pruning or tying down. After year 5, the central leader is generally controlled by cutting to a competing lateral on 2-, 3-, or 4-year-old wood. Bending over the leader is not recommended.

The same principles as outlined above are employed throughout the life of the mature slender spindle orchard. Special caution is advised concerning the vigor of the tree, particularly at the top third of the canopy. The growth **must** remain weak and must be continually renewed after fruiting. If the top is allowed to become vigorous and dominant, the fruiting portion of the lower third of the tree is eliminated. All parts of the tree must receive light. Shading also reduces fruit quality.

FIGURE 2a. Upper scaffold renewal with "stubbing" cut. The fruiting branch is removed when it exceeds its allotted space or is shading out branches below it. A short stub (about 1 inch) is left; a new branch is allowed to grow from the stub and become the new fruiting branch.

More research remains to be conducted under warm desert conditions to better understand the proper amount of lateral growth to decrease sunburn problems, especially on sensitive varieties such as Granny Smith and Jonagold.

The slender spindle system, as described above, is the "pure" system. Modifications of the system will be devised to fit Pacific Northwest growing conditions. The higher light incidence and longer growing season in a desert climate, as compared to the Netherlands where the system was developed, will certainly mean that we must adapt the slender spindle system for our needs and purposes. A taller slender spindle tree (8 feet) would utilize light efficiently under Pacific Northwest growing conditions.

FIGURE 2b. Limb shortening is accomplished by pruning to a weak lateral or, preferably, a fruiting lateral. This type of pruning cut is used as a containment cut.

It may be necessary to use more heading into 1-year-old wood than the original slender spindle system allows. Treatment of the leader may be modified to light tipping on varieties such as Granny Smith, which may require more feathery growth at the top of the canopy, and tying, rather than heading, for devigoration.

Vertical axis system

The "axe centrale," or vertical axis tree training system, was developed by Lespinasse in the 1970's. It is a central leader tree trained to a 3- or 4-wire trellis. Modifications of the trellis have been successfully employed, such as a 1-wire trellis with bamboo stakes for individual tree support. Generally, trees are 10 to 14 feet high, depending on the rootstock used, and about 5 to 6 feet wide. Rootstocks range from M 9 to MM 111 under French conditions, with MM 111 recommended for severe replant sites. Tree density ranges from 500 to 600 trees per acre. Trees are usually planted in single rows, as opposed to the multi-row bed system used frequently with the slender spindle. The tree has a narrow pyramid shape, with an open (sparse top. *(See Table 1).*

TRAINING THE VERTICAL AXIS TREE

Year 1 – at planting: If unbranched trees ("whips") are planted, it is advisable to head the tree 30 to 33 inches above the ground to force lateral branching. Preferably, branched or feathered trees are utilized. As originally described, heading of the central leader is not done. It may be advisable to head the leader 10 to 12 inches above the highest retained branch. This type of heading cut encourages the development of a strong, permanent lower tier of branches. As with the slender spindle, branches that have poor angles, or that are lower than 18 inches above the soil line, are removed.

Year 1 – summer: Limb positioning is an important aspect of tree training for the vertical axis. Weights and strings are most commonly used. In a non-spur variety, branches can be trained to the horizontal. For a spur type, a more moderate branch angle, i.e., 45 to 60 degrees, is advised.

Early summer pruning is an essential part of tree training. Branches that are overly vigorous or with narrow angles are completely removed (thinning cuts) in May and June, when 3 to 6 inches long. In fact, if rigorous summer pruning is conducted, little or no dormant pruning is required the subsequent winter. *(See Figure 4.)*

The leader must be supported by tying it to the supporting pole. Plastic tubing and tape are commonly used. Nylon string is not advised, because of risks of girdling the leader.

Year 2 – dormant pruning: No dormant pruning is required if summer pruning has been utilized. If no summer pruning was done, remove competing laterals, vigorous upright growth, low branches, and poorly placed growth. The leader is not headed.

Year 2 – summer training and pruning: Tree training and pruning techniques are identical to those used for year 1. Caution: do not allow vigorous growth to remain on the tree. *(See Figure 3).* The most desirable wood to be retained is weak horizontal growth.

Year 3 – dormant pruning: Remove uprights and vigorous branches. The central leader is not headed. Very little pruning should be required.

Year 3 – summer training and pruning: As in the previous two summers, special attention must be paid to eliminate overly vigorous fruiting branches. In addition, the vigor of the top of the tree must be controlled. One of the easiest methods of controlling top vigor is to let the leader bend over above the

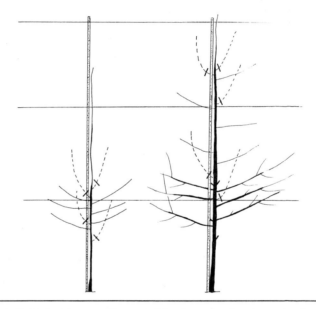

FIGURE 3. First and second leaf vertical axis-trained trees showing the use of thinning-out cuts ("pinching") during the summer. Vigorous uprights and poorly placed branches are removed to aid in tree training and reduce the amount of dormant pruning (after Barritt, 1988).

point of central leader support with the weight of cropping. Later, the portion of the central leader above the support that has become pendulant is removed entirely. This process will likely be repeated in subsequent years.

It is important to remove strong upright growth at the top of the tree; this growth can interfere with fruit bud formation in the bottom portion of the tree.

Year 4 – dormant pruning: The lower scaffolds are permanent branches and must eventually be shortened. Shortening to lateral branches is used to contain the lower scaffold branches to their allotted space. Also, the weight of the crop bends the branches downward, and so branches are pruned to promote a more horizontal growth habit. *(See Figure 4)*.

Vigorous growth is removed, and replacement branches are selected in the upper portion of the tree. If a branch has fruited and requires replacement, an angled stub is made. *(See Figures 2a and 4)*. A new branch will emerge from adventitious buds and can then replace the old branch.

Pruning the mature vertical axis tree employs the same techniques as that of the slender spindle:

1) The lower permanent scaffold branches are shortened to weak lateral branches (preferably fruiting laterals) to contain their length.

2) The upper two-thirds of the canopy receive renewal pruning. Fruiting laterals are not allowed to remain in the tree for more than 3 or 4 years. Constant renewal of the fruiting wood is critical to keep the mature vertical axis tree productive.

3) Light must reach every portion of the tree. If light is limiting, production will be affected. Special care must be taken to keep the top of the tree weak to prevent shading in the bottom section of the tree.

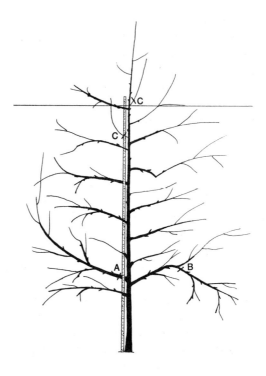

FIGURE 4. Fourth or fifth leaf vertical axis-trained apple tree:
a) removal of lower scaffold fruiting branch which is too
vigorous and has exceeded its allotted space. The limb removal is
conducted during the dormant season; b) shortening of a lower
fruiting branch which has become pendant. The droopy growth
is removed to a younger, more horizontal branch; c) removal of
vigorous uprights which compete with the leader. This pruning
is conducted in the summer, preferably when the shoots are 4 to 6
inches long (after Barritt, 1988).

110

In conclusion

Both the slender spindle and the vertical axis training systems are central leader systems. There is a dependence on summer pruning for tree training (limb positioning) and a lack of heading into 1-year-old wood. Renewal pruning and limb shortening are critical to the success of these systems. The systems differ in how the central leader is handled. With the slender spindle tree, the central leader is headed into 2-year-old wood (or older) to a replacement lateral which is tied upward to continue the central leader. In contrast, the vertical axis leader is never headed, except at planting.

Modifications of these 2 systems will certainly be required for the warm, high light intensities that exist in the Pacific Northwest. We are concerned with sunburn on varieties such as Granny Smith and Jonagold. It is likely we may grow taller trees than those used in Europe, and we may need to leave more weak growth in the tree to shade the fruit.

Both the slender spindle and vertical axis systems will produce more quickly – if handled correctly – than the traditional PNW central leader system. In addition to earlier production is the advantage of improved labor efficiency. Changing to high density systems in the Pacific Northwest will not be a matter of "if," but "when."

Additional reading

Barritt, B.H. 1984. Central leader training systems for apples. *Good Fruit Grower* 35(21):56-61.

Barritt, B.H. 1986. Reducing tree size and controlling excess growth. *Good Fruit Grower* 37(21):88, 90, 92.

Barritt, B.H. 1988. Vertical axis training seen as alternative for apples. *Good Fruit Grower* 39(3):24-26.

Peterson, A.B. and B.H. Barritt. 1986. European tree training techniques. *Good Fruit Grower* 37(20):5-7.

Wertheim, S.J. 1980. High density planting: development and current achievements in Netherlands, Belgium and West Germany. *Acta Horticulturae* 114:318-327.

Wertheim, S.J. 1978. Pruning of slender spindle type trees. *Acta Horticulturae* 165:173-179.

Lespinasse, J.M. 1981. Apple tree management in flat, vertical axis and palmette forms, by cultivar fruiting type. Experiments with other species: plum, peach, pear, and cherry. In: Perspectives de l'horticulture arbres fruitiers et petits fruits. *Colloques Scientifiques*, Les Floralies Internationales de Montreal. 15:27-130.

Tukey, L.D. 1988. Experiences with the French axe. *Compact Fruit Tree* 21:16-19.

Granger, R.L. and P. Philion 1988. Modifications in the French vertical axis system of apple trees. *Compact Fruit Tree* 21:20-23.

Maillard, A. and P. Herman. 1988. Development and management of trees in our version of the vertical axe system in Castang. *Compact Fruit Tree* 21:23-35.

7 SUPPORT SYSTEMS FOR HIGH DENSITY ORCHARDS

By K. Bert van Dalfsen

HIGH DENSITY ORCHARD PLANTINGS OF DWARF AND SEMI-DWARF fruit trees are a growing trend in the Pacific Northwest. Dwarf trees produce fruit faster and in less space than standard trees. However, very dwarf trees have poor root anchorage and must be supported. Semi-dwarf trees require support systems for training methods that control vigor. The support system also provides greater exposure to sunlight, thus increasing fruit yield, quality, and uniformity. The small trees also make spraying, pruning, and picking much easier.

Support systems for orchards can be traced back thousands of years. The Hanging Gardens of Babylon were actually supported by masonry walls. New materials have also become available since the first trellises were built in the Pacific Northwest. Today, pressure-treated posts and galvanized high-tensile wire are available to build durable support systems at a reasonable cost. The support system must be built to last, because the support is an integral part of the planting. If the post, wire, or anchors fail in a support system, the deteriorated or broken trellis can be difficult or impossible to repair. The support failure can lead to growth problems, reducing production and depreciating the entire investment.

Pressure-treated posts

To maximize the life of a support system, buy posts that have been pressure-treated with wood-preserving chemicals. While treated wood costs slightly more, pressure-treated posts pay for themselves in greatly reduced system maintenance and extended life. When purchasing pressure-treated posts, request posts that have been treated according to the appropriate standard for "ground contact" conditions.

There are three major chemicals used by pressure-treating plants. These are creosote, pentachlorophenol (PCP), and chromated copper arsenate (CCA). Creosote and PCP are not soluble in water, so they are usually dissolved or diluted in a petroleum-based solvent, such as light oil, for pressure treatment purposes. The oil is used as a "carrier" to assist in the penetration of the preservative in a spaced stack of timber when it is heated and pressurized in a large steel cylinder or "retort."

Posts treated with creosote or oil-impregnated pentachlorophenol may cause damage to rootstocks. One source suggests keeping tree rootstocks 18 inches away from the posts at the soil line. If a volatile solvent such as naptha or ethylene dichloride is used, the solvent will be reclaimed by evaporation under vacuum, and only the colorless crystals of PCP remain in the wood.

CCA, on the other hand, is a combination of water-soluble salts dissolved in water and forced into the wood. They are thought to combine chemically with the wood, resulting in little or no loss on subsequent contact with humidity, rain, and groundwater. Ammoniacal copper arsenate (ACA) is another salt-type preservative, which is used to a lesser degree than CCA. ACA, however, has been reported to cause corrosion in contact with trellis wire.

Fortunately, CCA pressure-treated posts are readily available, as they are considered the best choice.

If a home treatment is to be used, for safety reasons do not use PCP. CCA is not effective in a home treatment. The best chemical for use in home treatment methods is copper naphthenate. This is the one oil-based preservative recommended for greenhouse use. Wood treated with copper naphthenate should be allowed to "weather" for at least one week after treatment before placing plants near the wood. This time period apparently allows the evaporation of its petroleum-based solvents.

POST INSTALLATION

There are a number of factors to be considered in the installation of posts, such as depth of set, soil type, soil moisture, and post installation method (driven or augered). By increasing the depth of set of a post by a third, the post's resistance to overturning will be doubled. Likewise, a driven post has one and one-half times the resistance to overturning as does one placed in an oversized hole and the earth rammed back around it. Soil types have differing effects on the post's resistance to overturning. Normally, sandy soils have less resistance than clays. Similarly, the wetter the soil, the lower the load required to overturn the post.

Handsetting versus driven posts When handsetting posts (in an oversized hole), always place the large end down. When driving posts, always place the small end down. Augering pilot holes 1 to 2 inches smaller in diameter than the post will facilitate driving blunt, larger diameter, and longer posts. The pilot hole can also be used to guide end posts that are to be driven at an angle.

For small diameter posts, a weighted section of pipe with a cap and handles could be used to drive the posts. To facilitate the manual driving of posts, a pilot hole could be formed using a soil probe through which water is forced under pressure via a sprayer pump and tank. Portable gas-powered two-man augers are also available to drill pilot holes. Post drivers that operate from a tractor's hydraulic system are the standard equipment used to install fence posts. The hydraulic post drivers are available in either three-point hitch mounts or trailer-mounted. Extensions to the driving ram will be required to drive posts which are longer than nine feet. Some contractors have mounted hydraulic drivers on front-end loaders to increase the range of post lengths that can be driven.

High-tensile wire

While high-tensile strength steel has been used in wire for many years, it has only been recently marketed in its current form for use in trellises and fences. Using high-tensile (HT) wire will increase trellis life and reduce maintenance. The main advantage of high-tensile strength steel is that it has more strength per unit cost than low-tensile strength steel. Considering the wire's physical and mechanical properties, the optimum size of the trellis wire appears to be 12½-gauge (0.10 in diameter). Larger diameter wires have extra weight and higher cost per meter, while smaller wires have shorter resistance to atmospheric corrosion. The wire should have a minimum tensile strength of 180,000 pounds per square inch and a minimum breaking strength of 1,380 pounds.

To maximize the wire's life, the wire must be galvanized. The type of galvanizing or the weight of zinc coating deposited on the wire can greatly affect its useful life. The suggested type of galvanizing for trellis wire is Class 3 or 0.80 ounce of zinc per square foot of wire surface. Table 1 shows types of galvanization, and Table 2 describes the approximate protection afforded by galvanization.

To fasten the wire to the post, 1¾ inch long, 9-gauge staples should be used. These staples have 50 percent more resistance to pull-out than 1½ inch long staples. For maximum holding power, staples should have slash-cut points. Staples with single legs or diamond-shaped points are not recommended. Staples should also be galvanized.

Staples should never be driven vertically into wood posts with both legs parallel to the wood grain. Doing so can split the post and reduce holding power. Rotating the staples off vertical to straddle the grain has greater resistance to pull-out. To maximize their holding power, staples should be driven so that their legs curve outward and not inward. Note that the slash-cut points act as wedges, which force the legs to curve away from the flat surfaces of the points as the staples are driven into the wood.

On rises, dips, or some end posts, where there is great upward or downward pressure of the trellis wires on the staple, double stapling will provide greater resistance to pull-out. Also, angling the staple downward or upward against the direction of

---

TABLE 1. Minimum weights of zinc coating on wire.

Wire size (gauge no.)	Amount of galvanizing (Minimum coating) (oz. of zinc per sq. ft. of wire surface)		
	Class 1	Class 2	Class 3
9	.40	.60	.80
11	.30	.50	.80
12½	.30	.50	.80
14½	.20	.40	.60

---

pull, adds to effectiveness. **Staples must never be driven home.** This will kink and weaken the wire and damage the zinc coating.

HT wire is less ductile than the low-tensile strength wire used in the past. This characteristic makes the wire more difficult to splice. Australian Wire Industries carried out an investigation into the performance of the various knots commonly used in fencing. The most effective knots tested failed at between 60 to 66 percent of the HT wire's breaking strength.

To maximize the strength of the HT wire splice, mechanical devices should be used. Three commercially available mechani-

118

cal splices proved to be effective in tests at British Columbia Institute of Technology (BCIT), including the Nicopress, Wire-link, and the Vineline. Other manufacturers' splices may also be effective, however, be sure to buy from a reputable dealer or have the splice tested to determine its strength. More details on the BCIT tests are available from Engineering Note 316.122-1, which is available from the B.C. Ministry of Agriculture and

TABLE 2. Approximate protection given wire by Class 1 and Class 3 galvanizing.[1]

Wire size (gauge no.)	Years until rust appears Climatic condition						Years after rust appears until wire reaches half strength Climatic condition		
	Dry		Humid		Coastal & Industrial		Dry	Humid	Coastal & Industrial
	Class 1	3	Class 1	3	Class 1	3			
9	15	30	8	13	3	6	50 +	50 +	25
11	11	30	6	13	2	6	50 +	50 +	16
12½	11	30	6	13	2	6	50 +	50 +	12
14½	7	23	5	10	1.5	4.5	50	20	7

Fisheries offices. Also available is a "Suppliers' List" for HT wire and accessories.

The HT wire, because of its mechanical properties, springs back when a wire is cut. To avoid kinks when dispensing the wire, a pay-out device such as the "spinning jenny" should be used to uncoil the wire in reverse order to the way the wire was coiled in manufacture.

One last suggestion when working with HT wire, which will simplify construction and maintenance, is to install the

TABLE 3. Anchor specifications: diameter (inches) by length (feet).

Trellis	Tie-back brace		Single-span brace (driven)[1]			Stay brace assembly		
	End post	Tie-back post	End post	Brace post	Horizontal brace	End post	Stay	Stay block
6 ft. vertical	4"x9'	5"x7'	5"x8'	4"x9'	4"x8'	5"x10'	3"x8'	5"x2½'
8 ft. vertical	4"x12'	5"x7'	5"x8'	4"x12'	4"x10'	5"x12'	4"x10'	5"x3½'
10 ft. vertical	5"x14'	5"x8'[2]	6"x8'	5"x14'	5"x12'	6"x14'	5"x12'	6"x4'
French axe	5"x14'	5"x8'[2]	6"x8'	5"x14'	5"x12'	6"x14'	5"x12'	6"x4'
Tatura	5"x14'[2]	N/A	N/A	N/A	N/A	N/A	N/A	N/A

[1] A single-span brace assembly with augered posts has the same brace post and horizontal brace post size as the driven assembly. The end post size should be increased to the size used in the stay brace assembly.

[2] The tie-back post must be driven 5 feet or set in a 5 feet deep augered hole.

N/A – Brace assembly is "not appropriate" for the trellis design.

wire, then pull it only hand-tight before tying it off. Use one of several "in-line tensioners" to take the wire up to full tension of 250 pounds. These are permanently installed in the trellis wire, which will allow the retensioning of wire when post movement slackens the wire. If a break should occur, the tensioner could be relaxed, the broken ends lapped, and a splice installed. When the wire is pulled too tight before the tensioner is installed, it will not be possible to lap any breaks, and repairs will require two splices.

These materials and methods are described in more detail in U.S. Steel's publication, "How to Build Orchard and Vineyard Trellises," and is available from some trellis materials suppliers.

Importance of wire anchors

In a trellis, the wires play the important role of carrying the weight of the fruit-laden trees. These wires must be securely anchored. Inadequate anchors would appear to be the most common failure of early orchard trellises in the Okanagan area of British Columbia.

There are several factors influencing the load on trellis wires. The strength and vigor of the rootstock, as well as the method of tree training, will determine the relative proportion of load carried by the tree and the wire. The weight of fruit production itself will be the most significant part of the load carried by each wire. Finally, the trellis post spacing will also affect the amount of wire sag and tension. When comparing trellises, be sure to consider all the factors affecting trellis loads, including rootstock, training methods, fruit production, and post spacing.

To complicate matters further, the load of each wire must be transferred to the ground. The greater the load or higher the wire, the more difficult it will be to anchor. The condition and strength of the soil will also affect the type of anchor chosen.

Until actual wire tension measurements in loaded trellises are available to determine anchor requirements, consider the following factors when selecting an anchor and comparing anchor requirements in different trellis designs:

1) Root and tree strength; how much load will they carry?
2) The tree training system; is the tree trained to the wire and is the whole tree supported, or only the leader?
3) The post spacing; the greater the spacing, the more sag and wire tension. With 12½-gauge HT wire, use post spacings of 30 to 50 feet, depending on apple and tree load.
4) Wire strength; ultimately, the wire can safely carry a

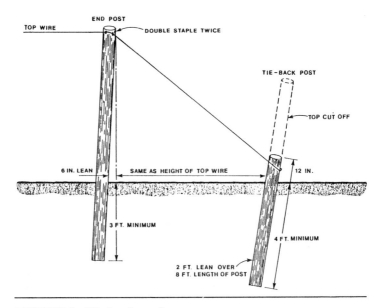

FIGURE 1. Tie-back anchor.

tension of about 1,000 pounds before it is permanently stretched. If in doubt about actual load, assume each wire carries 1,000 pounds.

Remember that anchor failure may be difficult to repair and may cause a lot of headaches in your production system. Be sure to prevent as many problems as possible with proper anchor selection and installation.

If you have difficult soil conditions for post installation, you may wish to compare trellis designs to determine which is easiest to install successfully in your orchard. Table 3, "Anchor Specifications," provides preliminary specifications for trellis designs described later in this chapter.

There are two types of anchors that are commonly used in trellises. One is a tie-back style using a wooden post or commer-

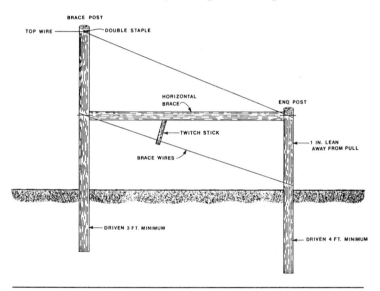

FIGURE 2. Single span brace assembly driven end post.

cially manufactured earth screws, metal plates, "arrowheads," or "duckbills." The other type of anchor is a brace assembly of three posts, two vertical and one horizontal, and a diagonal brace wire.

Figure 1 depicts a tie-back post anchor. The post should be driven at a backwards angle of 2 feet in 8 feet and 4 to 5 feet deep. The post can then be cut off at a height of 1 foot above the ground-line. (Post drivers cannot drive the top of the post within 1 foot of the ground). The post at ground-line should be positioned as far back from the end post as the top wire is high. The tie-back post must be driven in undisturbed firm soils to be effective. If the loads are too great (large number of wires), or the soils are weak, a brace assembly should be used. Commercial tie-back

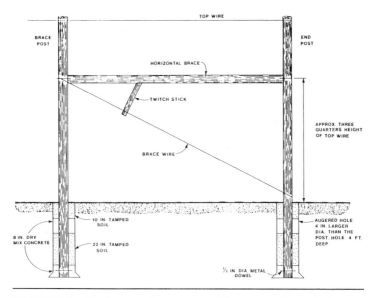

FIGURE 3. Single span brace assembly augered post holes.

124

anchors must also be placed in undisturbed soil.

A single-span brace assembly with a driven end post is shown in Figure 2. An 8-foot end post is chosen, because it can be driven by most post drivers. The size of the end post and length of horizontal brace should be increased as the height of the trellis and number of trellis wires increase. The U.S. Steel manual, "How to Build Orchard and Vineyard Trellises," describes the constuction method in detail. The end post depth is critical to the strength of this brace assembly. It is worth the extra effort to pull and reinstall end posts where required, to obtain the required depth. Increasing the length of the horizontal brace lowers the angle of the diagonal brace wire, reducing the lifting force on the end post and increasing the strength of the brace assembly.

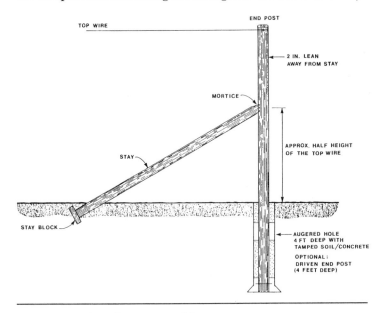

FIGURE 4. Stay brace assembly.

If the end post cannot be driven, then the brace assembly shown in Figure 3 should be used. The end post may be placed by using a tractor-mounted auger to make a hole that is 4 inches larger than the diameter of the post and 4 feet deep. The post is placed and centered in the hole. Pour and tamp concrete mix to a depth of 8 inches, then place and tamp 22 inches of soil. Add another 8 inches of concrete mix and 10 inches of soil. To attain maximum compaction, fill and compact only small amounts of soil at a time. If soil moisture is adequate, dry pre-mixed con-

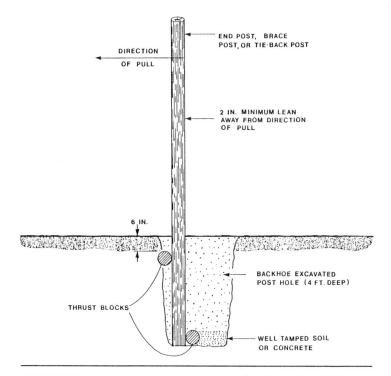

DIRECTION OF PULL

END POST, BRACE POST, OR TIE-BACK POST

2 IN. MINIMUM LEAN AWAY FROM DIRECTION OF PULL

6 IN.

THRUST BLOCKS

BACKHOE EXCAVATED POST HOLE (4 FT. DEEP)

WELL TAMPED SOIL OR CONCRETE

FIGURE 5. Supporting posts placed in backhoe-dug holes.

126

crete may be placed in the hole. The soil moisture will then set the concrete. Ready-mix concrete may also be used.

Filling the hole completely with ready-mix concrete is not significantly stronger than the layered concrete mix and soil tamped backfill already described. A one-half inch dowel of

TABLE 4. Vertical trellis design.

Materials	Component measures (in)		
	6 ft[1]	8 ft[2]	10 ft[3]
End posts - diameter	4-5	4-5	5-6
- length	108	144	168
- depth in-ground	36	48	48
In-line posts - diameter	3-4	3-4	4-5
- length	96	120	144
- depth in-ground	24	24	24
Distance between posts (ft)	30-50	30-50	30-50
Distance between wires			
ground to 1	24	36	36
1 to 2	24	24	24
2 to 3	24	18	24
3 to 4	—	18	18
4 to 5	—	—	18
Distance between trees (ft)	6	7	8
Distance between rows (ft)	13	14	15

[1]See Figure 6.　　[2]See Figure 7.　　[3]See Figure 8.

re-bar should be driven through a hole augered in the bottom of the post to fix the post to the concrete. A bell shape in the bottom of the hole also helps to prevent uplift.

A "stay" brace assembly is shown in Figure 4. This brace can be used with a driven end post or an augered end post fixed in concrete. The New Zealanders have a method of anchoring the end post without concrete. In this design, the diagonal stay is placed approximately halfway between the ground and the top of the end post. The stay block requires only a shallow trench. This may be an advantage if there are too many rocks in the soil for a post-hole auger.

Field practice in some areas of exremely rocky soil conditions is often to use a backhoe to dig the post holes. In these circumstances, the posts require extra support, as the soil cannot be adequately tamped in these large holes. To provide this support, thrust blocks should be placed on the appropriate sides of the post near the top and at the bottom of the hole, as shown in Figure 5.

In different soil conditions, there is also a tendency to pour concrete in dug holes to anchor the trellis. Unless the concrete anchor is supported by undisturbed soil, it is not likely to have sufficient mass to anchor the trellis wire. For example, 12½-gauge HT wire has a breaking strength of approximately 1,500 pounds. A 10-cubic-foot, reinforced concrete block could be lifted by a single trellis wire!

Support system designs

Numerous support systems have been used successfully for commercial tree fruit production around the world. However, for every system that has been developed, there are dozens of grower adaptations. This presents a problem when attempting to describe a given system. To avoid confusion, the support systems described herein should be considered the base models for each design.

Four support systems show potential for tree fruit production in the Pacific Northwest. They are the:

1) vertical trellis;
2) vertical (French) axis;
3) Tatura trellis; and
4) slender spindle.

Other systems, such as the Ebro Espalier and Lincoln canopy, must be ruled out at this time, due to their excessive start-up costs. In the Pacific Northwest, most apple growers are utilizing the freestanding central leader system. Over the years, these trees have served growers well. However, initial dollar returns have been greatly delayed due to rootstock characteristics and the very nature of the training system. Increasing costs make it critical that new plantings come into bearing quickly.

VERTICAL TRELLIS

Vertical trellises of different heights are currently being used throughout North America with a great deal of success. Common trellis heights are 6, 8, and 10 feet. Although 4-foot trellises are used, the necessity of using the unproven M 27 rootstock eliminates it from further discussion on a commercial basis.

Due to varying load factors, all trellises do not require materials of the same stature. Table 4 outlines the requirements of each.

Trees grown on a vertical trellis can be trained in many ways. Perhaps the most popular training systems are:

1) Horizontal palmette (branches emanating at 90 degrees from the leader and trained to the wires);

2) Oblique palmette or "Pennsylvania State Low Trellis Hedgerow" (45 degrees); and

3) Van Roechoudt palmette.

Many training systems have potential on a trellis, provided one principle is strictly adhered to. Vigor must be maintained in the lower scaffolds and reduced towards the top of the trellis. This point applies to all trees grown with a central leader.

It is very important to construct a sound trellis system. Anchors that pull out, poles that snap or rotate in the soil, staples that pull out, or wires that stretch with expansion and contraction, can seriously harm the current season's crop, as well as restrict future performance of the trees.

A vertical trellis support system can be used successfully with apples, pears, prunes, plums, and peaches. With peaches, it may be difficult to justify the cost of a trellis, since they bear quickly when freestanding.

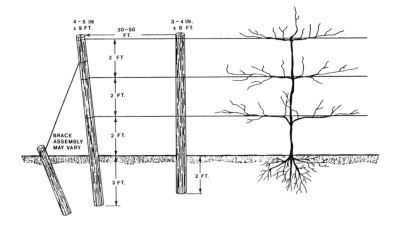

FIGURE 6. Six-foot trellis.

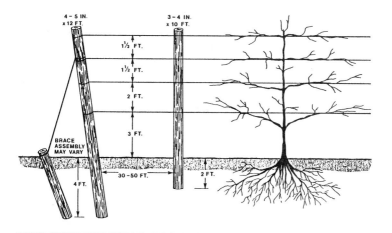

FIGURE 7. Eight-foot trellis.

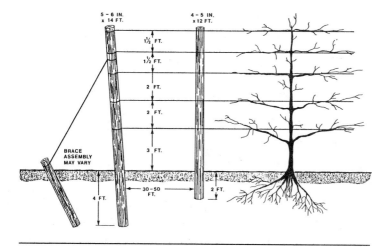

FIGURE 8. Ten-foot trellis.

VERTICAL (FRENCH) AXIS

The vertical axis support system is very similar to the 10-foot trellis. Table 5 lists the necessary structural components.

The vertical axis support system lends itself nicely to grower adaptations. Post size and placement should not vary; however,

TABLE 5. Vertical axis design.

Materials	Component measures (in)
End posts - diameter	5-6
- length	168
- depth in-ground	48
In-line posts - diameter	4-5
- length	144
- depth in-ground	24
Distance between posts (meters)	30-50
Distance between wires	
ground to 1	12
1 to 2	53
2 to 3	53
Distance between trees (ft)	4
Distance between rows (ft)	15

from one to five wires can be used for crop support. Bamboo sticks, thin posts, wire, string, and other materials have been used as leader supports. Trees trained to this system are never headed, when growing properly; consequently, the leader will devigorate if allowed to flop over with fruiting. For this reason, it is important to select a leader support that will last and withstand the stresses cropping puts on it.

The vertical axis system shown in Figure 9 depicts a 3-wire trellis with full-length leader support at each tree, securely fastened to all 3 wires. This will provide the most cost-effective trellis. It is not critical for the leader support to extend past the bottom wire into the ground.

At this time, apples are the only tree fruit crop considered for use with this support system.

TATURA TRELLIS

An Australian system, the Tatura, was designed to increase the bearing surface of the vertical trellis system. Table 6 is a listing of the trellis specifics.

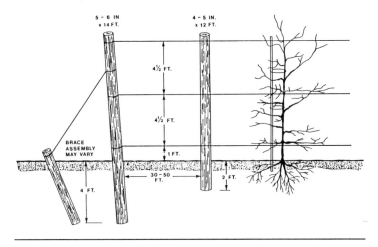

FIGURE 9. Vertical French axis.

As seen in Figure 10, this support system utilizes crossed support posts, forming a vee-shaped trellis. Ten wires are fastened to the posts (5 per side), and cross braces are affixed between the tips of all end post pairs. Cross braces are optional for in-line post pairs. The trees are headed at 24 inches to produce double

TABLE 6. Tatura trellis design.

Materials	Component measures (in)
End posts - diameter	5-6
- length	192
- depth in-ground	48
In-line Posts - diameter	4-5
- length	144
- depth in-ground	24
Cross braces - diameter	3-4
- length	120
Distance between posts (ft)	30-50
Distance between wires	
ground to 1	36
1 to 2	24
2 to 3	24
3 to 4	18
4 to 5	18
Distance between trees (ft)	6
Distance between row middles (ft)	17

leaders. The leaders are then trained to the wires on opposite sides of the trellis.

Support posts of the Tatura are pounded in at a 60-degree angle to the horizontal. This produces a 60-degree angle between the 2 posts as well. The juncture of the 2 posts (bottom of the vee) is at 18 inches above the ground in a 10-foot Tatura trellis. The nature of the angled cropping system, combined with the pull of 10 wires under tension, places a great deal of stress on the entire

TABLE 7. Slender spindle design.

Materials	Component measures (in)
Posts - diameter	2
- length	96
- depth in-ground	24
Distance between posts (ft)	5
Distance between trees (ft)	5
Distance between rows (ft)	13

support system. Post sizes, use of cross braces, and anchor durability cannot be compromised with this system, if the structure is to remain intact for two decades.

The Tatura trellis is well suited to apples, pears, plums, and prunes. It may also be the best support system for peaches and Asian pears, where fruit movement must be kept to a minimum to reduce fruit scuffing. Cherries and apricots have been tried on the Tatura and other trellis systems with limited success. At this point, it would not be advisable to use a trellising system with cherries or apricots on any more than a trial basis.

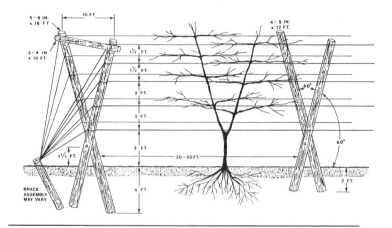

FIGURE 10. Tatura trellis.

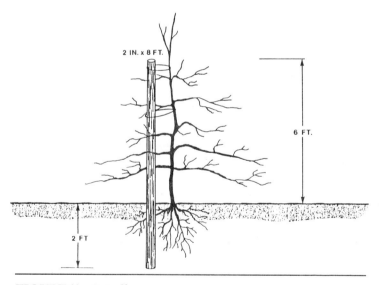

FIGURE 11. Spindle.

136

SLENDER SPINDLE

Figure 11 shows the simplicity of this support system. The slender spindle does not require large support posts, anchors, or wires. A slender 2-inch by 8-foot post is pounded 2 feet into the ground to support the leader and cropping tree. String wrapped around branches and tied down to a spike driven into the sup-

TABLE 8a. Summary of costs, based on 1986 prices for materials in British Columbia's Okanagan Valley.

Materials	Material cost (Canadian $)
POSTS	
2 to 3 inch x 8 feet	$ 1.60
3 to 4 inch x 8 feet	2.30
4 to 5 inch x 9 feet	4.25
3 to 4 inch x 10 feet	3.25
4 to 5 inch x 12 feet	6.00
4 to 5 inch x 14 feet	8.00
5 to 6 inch x 16 feet	15.00
Vertical axis leader pole	.50
Anchor[1]	5.00
½-inch bolt	1.00
WIRE	
12½-gauge HT wire, 3,330-ft. roll	70.00
HT wire tie-off splice	1.00
HT wire "in-line tensioner"	3.00

[1] *The same anchor cost was assumed for each trellis.*

port post at ground level is used to train most limbs. The leader can be zigzagged across the post to control leader vigor and promote lateral branching. Table 7 is a listing of slender spindle specifications.

This system is highly intensive, therefore, it is very important that a grower starts with a very strong, feathered nursery tree to assure early, heavy cropping.

The slender spindle system is best suited to apples. Growth and cropping habits of other tree fruits makes this system less desirable than a trellised system.

Support system costs

Tables listing the cost of the various support system designs have been prepared. These support system costs are based on 1986 prices for materials in British Columbia's Okanagan Valley. A summary of the material costs are:

Installation costs are also estimated. A local contractor installs wire for $50.00 per 3,330-foot roll. Post and anchor installation have been roughly estimated as a cost charged by contractors:

6-ft. Vertical trellis	$2.00/post or anchor
8-ft. Vertical trellis	$2.25/post or anchor
10-ft. Vertical trellis or Vertical axis trellis	$2.50/post or anchor
Slender spindle	$1.25/post
Tatura trellis	$7.50/"V" assembly
	$5.00/anchor

A uniform $6.00 per tree cost has been assumed. This, combined with the above information, allows for a tree and total

TABLE 8. Six-foot trellis.

Row spacing	13 ft	
Tree spacing	6 ft	
Trees per acre	558	
Costs ($ per acre)		
Trees $6.00 per tree		$3,350

Trellis materials (500-ft spans)	PER SPAN	PER ACRE
Wire (1,500 ft)	$31.50	
Splices	3.00	
Tensioners (3)	9.00	
Line posts (11)	25.30	
End posts (2)	9.50	
Anchors (2)	10.00	
Sub-total	$88.30	590
Installation (approx)		360
TOTAL (Canadian $)		$4,300

TABLE 9. Eight-foot trellis.

		PER SPAN	PER ACRE
Row spacing	14 ft		
Tree spacing	7 ft		
Trees per acre	444		
Costs ($ per acre)			
Trees $6.00 per tree			$2,660
Trellis materials (500-ft spans)			
Wire (2,000 ft)		$42.00	
Splices		4.00	
Tensioners (3)		12.00	
Line posts (11)		35.75	
End posts (2)		12.00	
Anchors (2)		10.00	
Sub-total		$115.75	720
Installation (approx)			410
TOTAL (Canadian $)			$3,790

TABLE 10. Ten-foot trellis.

		PER SPAN	PER ACRE
Row spacing	15 ft		
Tree spacing	8 ft		
Trees per acre	363		
Costs ($ per acre)			
Trees $6.00 per tree			$2,180
Trellis materials (500-ft spans)			
Wire (2,500 ft)		$52.50	
Splices		5.00	
Tensioners (5)		15.00	
Line posts (11)		66.00	
End posts (2)		18.00	
Anchors (2)		10.00	
Sub-total		$166.50	970
Installation (approx)			450
TOTAL (Canadian $)			$3,600

TABLE 11. Vertical axis.

	PER SPAN	PER ACRE
Row spacing	15 ft	
Tree spacing	4 ft	
Trees per acre	726	
Costs ($ per acre)		
Trees $6.00 per tree		$4,360
Trellis materials (500-ft spans)		
Wire (1,500 ft)	$31.50	
Splices	3.00	
Tensioners (3)	9.00	
Line posts (11)	66.00	
End posts (2)	18.00	
Anchors (2)	10.00	
Leader pole (125)	62.50	
Sub-total	$200.00	1,160
Installation (approx)		360
TOTAL (Canadian $)		$5,880

TABLE 12. Tatura.

	PER SPAN	PER ACRE
Row spacing	17 ft	
Tree spacing	6 ft	
Trees per acre	427	
Costs ($ per acre)		
Trees $6.00 per tree		$2,560
Trellis materials (500-ft spans)		
Wire (5,000 ft)	$105.00	
Splices	10.00	
Tensioners (10)	30.00	
Line posts (22)	176.00	
End posts (4)	60.00	
Cross ties (11)	35.75	
Anchors (4)	20.00	
Sub-total	$436.75	2,240
Installation (approx)		970
TOTAL (Canadian $)		$5,770

TABLE 13. Spindle.

Row spacing	13 ft
Tree spacing	5 ft
Trees per acre	670
Costs ($ per acre)	
Trees $6.00 per tree	$4,020
Materials (670 posts)	1,070
Installation (approx)	840
TOTAL (Canadian $)	$5,930

support system cost to be projected for each design. Installation of the trees has not been included in these numbers. These costs are tabulated in Tables 8 to 13 and summarized in Table 13.

TABLE 14. Cost summary per acre (Canadian $).

Support system	Trees	Support material	Support installation	Total
6-ft. trellis	$3,350	$ 590	$360	$4,300
8-ft. trellis	2,660	720	410	3,790
10-ft. trellis	2,180	970	450	3,600
Vertical axis	4,360	1,160	360	5,880
Spindle	4,020	1,070	840	5,930
Tatura	2,560	2,240	970	5,770

In conclusion

If properly treated and constructed, the support system will outlast the trees it is supporting. Many trellis and spindle plantings exist in North America that are 20 years old and producing large volumes of top-quality fruit.

These systems and the results they can produce are very attractive, however, the approach is much different from free-standing central leader training. Growers contemplating an intensive planting must be prepared to adopt new training and crop management ideas. Dr. Loren Tukey, professor of pomology, Pennsylvania State University suggests that "success depends upon a good match between the grower and the system and method used." Any system will work, if the grower is willing to spend the time and effort to make it work.

Growers considering installation of a support system can obtain further information by purchasing a copy of U.S. Steel's booklet, "How to Build Orchard and Vineyard Trellises."

Additional reading

United States Steel, 1982. How to Build Orchard and Vineyard Trellises. U.S.S. Catalogue No. T-111578, Pittsburg, Pennsylvania, U.S.A. 15230.

Schuler, Albert. Good Fencing is Good Farming - Part 2. New Zealand Wire Industries Limited, P.O. Box 22198, Auckland, New Zealand.

van Dalfsen, K.B. 1984. Splices for High-Tensile Smooth Fencing Wire. Engineering Note No. 316-122-1. B.C. Ministry of Agriculture and Fisheries.

Australian Wire Industries Pty. Ltd. 1982. Waratah Fence Manual. A.W.I. Pty. Ltd., 37 Pitt St., Sydney, N.S.W., Australia.

8 EFFECT OF TREE DENSITY ON PROFITABILITY

By H. George Geldart

THIS CHAPTER DISCUSSES INFORMATION DEVELOPED ON THE ECO-nomics of high density plantings for apples. The objective is to provide a quick summary of the differences between planting densities from an economic and financial perspective. The information is presented from a practical farm management point of view.

The orchard replant question is of concern to many growers, as margins shrink and pressure increases on maintaining efficient and profitable orchards. It is indeed a complex question and requires a thorough analysis of all pertinent factors. It is imperative that growers consider the impact of all variables in making the decision to replant. Such thorough analysis helps address the significant risk factors and the farm's ability to withstand the financial impact of various risks such as production levels and market returns. This chapter reviews economic information and integrates pertinent production and marketing factors through sensitivity analysis to assist farm managers in arriving at a decision with respect to alternative densities and production systems.

As part of this discussion, it is useful to put economics into perspective. The information available deals with various factors such as rootstocks, systems, spacing, cultivars, as well as economics. It is the economics that is the catalyst for change. All of the other factors impact economics and profitability. Therefore, all of these factors must be integrated in making an assessment of profitability for various planting densities of apples. The target is, after all, the improvement of the "bottom line."

In discussing the economics, it is useful to look at the decision to replant as a process. It can be broken into three parts: assessing the current situation, looking at alternatives, and deciding on alternatives. It is important to assess the current situation, and breakdown the orchard by variety or block. The first question to address is whether existing blocks are profitable;

148

that is, if the cashflow is positive or negative. If unprofitable blocks are identified, can their financial picture be improved upon through management practices, or are the varieties obsolete from a marketing perspective, with little optimism for improvement. The outcome of this process may lead to a review of alternatives to improve profitability. In addressing the economics, the following discussion is an assessment of the relative profitability of different apple planting densities and systems involved in the decision to replant.

This chapter is based primarily on a series of establishment cost budgets, which have been prepared from a computer spreadsheet model developed by the author. Six alternative densities and systems are discussed, and an estimation of the costs and returns over an 8-year period is provided. A further point here is that these are basically partial budgets; they look only at the alternative densities on 1 acre. Also, the figures are in Canadian dollars.

The main point or result from this analysis is that higher density systems are more profitable than low density systems, not withstanding risk variables. It should be stressed that there are three key profitability factors in the economics of high density plantings. In order of significance or impact they are:

1) price and quality;
2) timing of production and production levels; and
3) planting year costs.

They reflect both risk variables and management considerations. The price/quality factor is impacted by market conditions, varieties, site, and horticultural practices. The timing and level of production is impacted by tree quality, site, and horticultural practices. Planting year costs are affected primarily by the costs of the trees and system materials. The importance of these variables is evident from the discussion.

TABLE 1. Planting year cash costs.

System	Density (trees/acre)	at $5.50/tree $/acre	at $2.50/tree ($/acre)
Slender spindle (11 x 5)	808	9,404	6,980
Central axis (11 x 5)	808	9,404	6,980
Central axis (13 x 5.5)	600	7,788	5,988
Trellis (14 x 6)	515	7,128	5,583
Central leader (15 x 7.6)	380	4,341	3,201
Central leader (18 x 12)	202	2,958	2,352

Costs of planting and establishment

Table 1 summarizes the planting year cash costs for the six densities and systems at a cost of both $5.50 and $2.50 per tree. At $5.50 per tree, the planting year cash costs per acre range from $2,958 for the central leader system at a density of 202 trees per acre, up to $9,404 for both the slender spindle and central axis systems planted at a density of 808 trees per acre. As expected, there is basically a straight-line relationship between tree density and planting year cash costs.

This linear relationship is offset somewhat, beginning with the trellis system at 515 trees per acre, because of the costs related to system materials and labor. The impact of tree cost on planting year cash costs is greater with increasing densities. However, as will be evident further in this chapter, this is not as significant a factor in the relative profitability of alternative densities. Figure

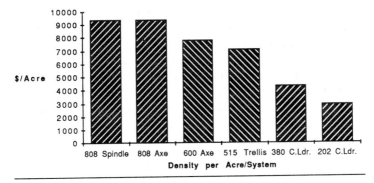

FIGURE 1. Planting year cash costs

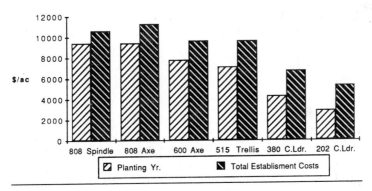

FIGURE 2. Planting year versus total establishment costs

1 provides another view of the planting year cash costs for these densities.

A further summary of the costs associated with these various densities is illustrated in Figures 2 and 3. The point here is that the planting year cash costs form the bulk of the total establishment costs for the higher densities than for the lower densities; on both a per-acre and per-tree basis (total establishment costs reflect the investment required in that they are the total of negative net cash income years for each density). For example, the 808 slender spindle planting shows that almost 90 percent of total establishment costs are planting year cash costs. For the 202 central leader planting, the planting year cash costs comprise roughly 50 percent. This illustrates a major difference between densities in that the period of time after the planting year before gross returns exceed cash expenses is greater for lower densities. This will become more evident further in the discussion.

High density production parameters

The timing and level of production used in the model is illustrated in Figure 4. The main point here is that the higher density systems produce more fruit earlier on. This, in fact, is the key to the profitability. The actual figures (bins/acre) are provided in Table 2. As can be seen from the numbers, the higher density systems reach their peak production earlier than the lower density systems. The total cumulative production for the 10-year period also measures the production advantage of these high density systems. These projected yields, based on information from horticulturists, show a range of total 10-year production, from 179.6 bins per acre for central leader 202, to 387.8 bins per acre for slender spindle 808.

152

Income versus costs

High production levels are directly related to high gross returns in high density plantings. This is depicted in Figures 5 and 6. Using an average return of $0.12 per pound ($100/bin) on all production, Figure 5 shows that the 202 tree

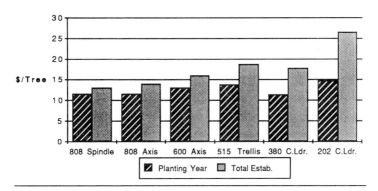

FIGURE 3. Per tree cash costs

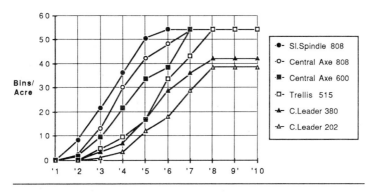

FIGURE 4. 10-year production estimates

TABLE 2. 10-year production estimates in bins (830 pounds) per acre.

Year	Slender spindle	Central axis	Central axis	Trellis	Central leader	Central leader
1	0.0	0.0	0.0	0.0	0.0	0.0
2	8.4	2.4	1.8	0.0	0.0	0.0
3	21.7	13.2	9.6	4.8	3.6	1.2
4	36.1	30.1	21.7	9.6	7.2	3.6
5	50.6	42.2	33.7	16.7	16.9	12.0
6	54.2	48.2	38.6	33.7	28.9	18.1
7	54.2	54.2	54.2	43.4	36.1	28.9
8	54.2	54.2	54.2	54.2	42.2	38.6
9	54.2	54.2	54.2	54.2	42.2	38.6
10	54.2	54.2	54.2	54.2	42.2	38.6
Total	387.8	352.9	322.2	270.8	219.3	179.6

per acre central leader did not generate sufficient income to cover the cash costs over the 8-year period. The higher density systems (600 trees per acre or more) generate more income than cash costs for the same period. Over the 12-year projection, shown in Figure 6, all densities generated enough total income to cover cash costs. However, it is significant to note that the excess of income over cash costs for the period is much greater for the higher densities.

Table 3 looks at the break-even prices for the various densities and systems over the 8-year budgeting period. This break-

TABLE 3. Break-even prices for 8-year totals.

System	at $5.50/tree ($/pound)	at $2.50/tree ($/pound)	at $7.00/tree ($/pound)
Slender spindle 808	0.0805	0.0710	0.0857
Central axis 808	0.0830	0.0730	0.0880
Central axis 600	0.0830	0.0756	0.0880
Trellis 515	0.1240	0.1110	0.1300
Central leader 380	0.1260	0.1156	0.1320
Central leader 202	0.1400	0.1320	0.1440

even price is the average return per pound required to cover all cash costs for the planting over the period. It is evident that, despite higher initial planting costs, the higher density systems have a lower required break-even price than the low densities. For $5.50 per tree costs in the planting year, the differential between slender spindle 808 and central leader 202 is nearly $0.06 per pound. Another point about this table is that the cost of the trees does not have a great impact on the break-even price. It is less than 1 cent per pound for both slender spindle 808 and central leader 202, if tree cost changes from $5.50 to $2.50. One conclusion here might be; do not skimp on tree cost. if it means not getting a high quality tree. It is the production level and quality of production from the tree that is important in order to generate a profit.

Table 4 looks at the impact of 8-year production levels on break-even prices. As is illustrated, a 25 percent reduction in overall yields has a significant impact on the price required to cover 8-year cash costs. In the case of slender spindle 808, the 25 percent reduction equates to an increase in break-even price of some 2.59 cents per pound. Looking at the other end of the scale, the same production decrease for 202 trees per acre on central leader increased break-even price by 4.6 cents per pound.

The payback period

The figures in Table 5 concern the payback period of the cash investment in each of these systems. The cash investment is simply the sum of the negative net cash incomes for the first few years. The payback period is then calculated (using

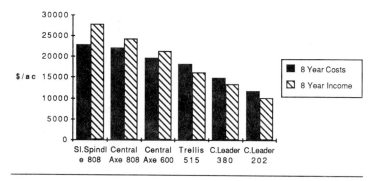

FIGURE 5. Summary of 8-year costs and income base ($0.12/lb.)

156

TABLE 4. 8-year production estimates: total pounds/acre and break-even price.

System	Production		Break-even price	
	Full	3/4	Full	3/4
Slender spindle 808	264,000	198,000	0.0805	0.1064
Central axis 808	254,000	190,500	0.0830	0.1100
Central axis 600	228,000	171,000	0.0830	0.1110
Trellis 515	134,000	100,500	0.1240	0.1650
Central leader 380	109,000	81,750	0.1260	0.1680
Central leader 202	84,000	63,000	0.1400	0.1860

an opportunity cost of cash invested of 6%) from the flow of positive net cash incomes from the planting. At the $0.12 per pound price, the higher density systems show the shortest payback period, with the 808 slender spindle planting at 6.8 years. Payback period gradually increases from this point up to 8.9 years for the 202 central leader planting.

The range of returns per pound show the impact of price on the payback period. As would be expected, the lower the average price on total tonnage, the longer the payback period. Although the relative difference is the same between densities, the price change impacts the payback period more on the low density system. Using the 202 and 808 comparison again: the reduction from $0.12 per pound to $0.10 per pound increases the payback period by 4.8 years on 202 central leader and only 2.6 years on 808 slender spindle. This, perhaps, illustrates the ability of high-producing systems to withstand a greater degree of price or market risk.

The gross margin

The gross margin is the difference between total income from a crop and total direct expenses associated with the production of that crop. In the case of these budgets, it is the total expected income from the projected tonnage of apples produced, less all direct costs associated with the establishment and production of these various densities and systems. Another way to view the gross margin is to consider it a contribution margin; that is, how much the crop contributes to the overall profitability of the orchard.

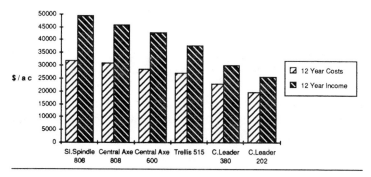

FIGURE 6. 12-year cash costs and income comparison (income base $0.12/lb.)

TABLE 5. Payback period (years).

Price per lb.	Slender spindle 808	Central axis 808	Central axis 600	Trellis 515	Central leader 380	Central leader 202
0.10	9.4	10.6	10.1	12.1	13.7	13.7
0.12	6.8	8.1	8.1	8.9	8.8	8.9
0.14	5.4	6.4	6.7	8.4	7.9	8.3

Table 6 summarizes the gross margin for the first positive year of each of these densities. The higher density systems begin generating a positive gross margin earlier, with the slender spindle 808 planting generating $487 per acre in the third year, at an average return of $0.12 per pound. The three lower densities do not generate a positive gross margin until year 5. It is this early return that allows the higher density systems to payback their investment faster.

Table 6 also shows the impact of price changes on the first positive gross margin year. As was the case with other analysis, these budgets are fairly sensitive to the price variable. For example, a change in average return from $0.12 per pound to $0.14 per pound changes the gross margin for the slender spindle 808 from $487 per acre to $847 per acre. As you will recall from Table 5, it also significantly reduced the payback period. Of course, it also goes the other way when we look at the down side risk of price.

Another overview of the gross margin is provided in Table 7. The total gross margins over a 10-year period show the high density systems with a significant advantage over lower density ones in their contribution to overall orchard profitability. After pay-

TABLE 6. Gross margins: first positive year ($/acre).

System	@ $0.10/lb.		@ $0.12/lb.		@ $0.14/lb.	
	Year	$	Year	$	Year	$
Slender spindle 808	3	127	3	487	3	847
Central axis 808	4	876	4	1,376	3	31
Central axis 600	4	362	4	722	4	1,082
Trellis 515	5	64	5	344	5	624
Central leader 380	5	98	5	378	5	658
Central leader 202	6	51	5	166	5	366

ing associated cash costs of establishment, the slender spindle 808 density shows a projected gross margin total of $11,307 per acre at an average return of $0.12 per pound. The same return projections for the central leader 202 show a total of $2,103. At the $0.10 per pound projection, the three lowest density systems show a negative contribution margin. This illustrates quite clearly that the increased tonnage earlier on in high density systems provides a financial advantage over lower density systems.

TABLE 7. Gross margins: 10-year totals ($/acre).

System	at $0.10/lb. ($)	at $0.12/lb. ($)	at $0.14/lb. ($)
Slender spindle 808	4,867	11,307	17,747
Central axis 808	2,633	8,493	14,353
Central axis 600	2,467	7,817	13,167
Trellis 515	(285)	4,215	8,715
Central leader 380	(826)	2,814	6,454
Central leader 202	(877)	2,103	5,083

Net present value

A net present value approach was used to assess the relative profitablity of the various planting densities and systems, because of differences in the productive life and timing of production of these systems. Net present value reflects the present value of the stream of income and costs associated with an investment. It uses a formula that discounts future dollars from the present at some percentage determined by the analyzer. The main underlying basis is that a dollar today is worth more than a dollar one year from now.

Table 8 summarizes the net present value per acre, using a

TABLE 8. Net present values: 10 percent discount rate, 15-year planning horizon.

System	at $0.10/lb. ($)	at $0.12/lb. ($)	at $0.14/lb. ($)
Slender spindle 808	1,844	6,595	11,347
Central axis 808	304	4,656	9,007
Central axis 600	703	4,728	8,754
Trellis 515	(804)	2,689	6,181
Central leader 380	(892)	1,904	4,700
Central leader 202	(666)	1,682	4,030

15-year planning horizon and a 10 percent discount rate. The main point here is that, generally, the higher density systems have a greater net present value per acre than lower density systems; that is, they are more profitable. All the densities have a positive net present value at an average return of $0.12 per pound. Per acre values range from $1,682 for central leader 202 to $6,595 for slender spindle 808. As was the case with the total gross margin analysis, the three lower densities show a negative net present value, using a projected return of $0.10 per pound.

As mentioned earlier, economics helps assess the relative profitability of these various densities and systems. These net present values provide a ranking of profitability based on the assumptions used in the replant model. The greater the net present value, the more profitable the density.

In conclusion
Using the computer model to look at the impact of certain risk variables, it was evident that there are three key factors affecting profitability in high density planting systems. In order of significance or impact, they are: **price and quality, timing of production and production levels, and planting year costs.** They reflect both risk variables and management considerations. Reviewing the figures and tables in this chapter, it can be seen how these three variables affect the potential profitability of alternate densities.

These items are important in considering the replant options for an orchard. In the case of price/quality factors, an assessment of market, variety, site, and horticultural considerations is important. For the timing and level of yields, tree quality, site, and horticultural variables are important. Planting year cash costs are primarily influenced by the cost of trees and system costs.

All of these factors must be considered when looking at the economics of alternative densities for any orchard planting. In considering the impact, address the management parameters associated with each risk variable. The budgets used in this chapter include parameters which are as realistic as possible for the general situation. It is important to look at the specific situation, and make projections that reflect those specifics. Assessing the impact of the up and down sides of risks associated with these key variables is important in looking at the profitability of any density.

The decision to replant an orchard is a complex one, and all relevant factors need to be considered. This chapter has illustrated that the high density systems have a greater potential for profit than low density systems. From here, it is important to go to the next step of the process and look at the feasibility of any alternative being considered. The answer to the question, are high density apple systems profitable?, is yes. The next question that needs to be addressed is, is it affordable? In order to address this, a cash flow budget or forecast is required to help assess which alternatives are feasible, given the size of replant acreage in comparison to the total farm, the debt load situation, personal financial requirements, and the associated risk factors, such as price, tree quality, replant disease, frost, and so forth. In this way, a replant program can be developed that best fits with the overall farm objectives.

9 ADAPTING A

HIGH DENSITY

SYSTEM TO

YOUR NEEDS

By Paul Tvergyak, Jim Fleming,
Tom Auvil, and Garth Kunz

ONE OF THE MOST DIFFICULT TASKS THAT GROWERS FACE AS THEY move toward higher density plantings will be collecting enough good information to make wise decisions. Trips and tours to other parts of the world where these systems are "old hat" are very beneficial, but the principles observed in other fruit districts still have to be applied under sometimes very different conditions. The result is that we all find ourselves in an uncomfortable situation of being innovators without the ability to rely on traditional sources of information.

When we evaluate high density orchard systems, we find that they are a type of central leader training where pruning principles are still applicable. One of the best ways to evaluate a new orchard system would be to plant a small trial orchard and observe the results. Time spent waiting for a trial planting to provide you with answers could likely be more than compensated for later by saving mistakes on a larger planting.

If we observe the results of others who are already using one of the higher density systems, we can often get a better idea of what to expect in our own orchard. The following comments address grower experiences with higher density plantings, under different conditions.

GROWER EXPERIENCES:

Jim Fleming   One trellis system which was tried consisted of a single wire with a string between the wire and the base of each Granny Smith tree. The string was first tied to the wire, the knot secured from slipping with a dab of tree heal paint. The string was then stapled to the base of each tree, using a staple gun. The branches were tied to a horizontal position during the fall of the first leaf. The area of the trees between the double rows was similar to a Lincoln canopy with horizontally trained

166

branches. The vertical portion was a combination of slender spindle and French axe. This system worked well. The block produced 1,600 loose boxes per acre in the third leaf.

However, by the fifth leaf, there was too much shade. The trellis was then modified by installing a 10-foot crossarm at a height of 8 feet. New wire was strung from the ends of the cross-arms, and the trees were pulled over and attached to the new wire. This procedure allowed for good fruit size and production in the lower part of the tree. Sufficient crop support can become a problem with this system. If the limbs are allowed to droop from crop load during the summer, sunburn becomes an additional problem.

Another system consisted of a 12-foot steel T-bar, driven in the ground 2 feet. At about 4 feet above ground, the post was bent out into the drive row to an angle of 30 degrees. After the third leaf, a piece of 5/8-inch steel was welded to the T-bar and bent to form an arch across the drive center. The wires started at 4 feet, then every 16 inches up the post. This method of trellis installation was too labor intensive.

A third system, somewhat similar to the first two systems described, was less labor intensive to install. Using an 18-foot T-bar driven 2 feet into the ground, the tops of the adjoining rows were welded together to form an A-frame. Wood posts are used on the end of each row for lateral strength. The wire on this system started at 40 to 48 inches from the ground and was spaced every 24 inches up the post to 12 feet. The goal with this system was to use the maximum amount of available light while providing enough shade to help prevent sunburn. In this new system, the trees were planted 5 feet apart at 1,000 trees per acre. The wire used for the trellis wss #12 high tensile (190,000 to 200,000 pound strength).

One key to a successful trellis system is the method used to anchor the system. As production increases near the top of the tree, much stress is placed upon the support system. Without adequate anchorage, the system will fail. Currently, Jim Fleming is using a 5 foot x 1/2 inch galvanized anchor rod. The anchor is a 6-inch expanding anchor. It will fit into a 6-inch augered hole. After it is placed at the bottom of the hole, a piece of 2-inch steel pipe is used to expand the anchor to a 12-inch diameter.

Limb positioning and minimum pruning are the most important elements in the development of a high density orchard. Maintenance of the system is done with whole limb removal of branches that become too large. Spur pruning in the bottoms of the trees also helps to maintain adequate vigor fruit quality. As tree numbers increase, it is important to use more dwarfing rootstocks. At planting, the bottom of the union should be at least 1 inch out of the ground. This will put the top of the rootstock 3 to 4 inches out of the ground and reduce the chance of scion rooting.

Tom Auvil　All training systems have advantages and disadvantages. High density systems have the potential to be very productive in the third or fourth season. If good management is used, the system can sustain substantially higher yields than we are accustomed to seeing. On the down side of high density are its high initial capital requirements and the increased risk in using new technology. High density systems are for growers who can learn and employ new concepts. There are examples of medium and high density orchards where all the elements of success are present, except the employment of vigor management. The most common mistake is pruning when training is required. Frequently, the pruning that is done consists of heading cuts, which causes the tree to grow suckers instead of forming fruit spurs. Heading delays production 2 years.

In the Lake Chelan area, growers are planting a mixture of freestanding and supported axe and spindle systems. Spur Delicious on M 7 or M 106 apparently will work in tree densities of

500 to 700 trees per acre, with spacing of 14x6 down to 12x5. Non-spur varieties need M 26 for best performance in the 500 to 700 trees per acre densities. M 9 will be most efficient on systems having 700 to 1,000 trees per acre for non-spur varieties, with spacings of 14x3 up to 12x5. M 9 rootstock is in short supply, requiring ordering of this rootstock 2 to 3 years in advance. The nurseries have been working at increasing supplies of M 9.

Key factors in the successful management of a high density orchard are: 1) planting large, well-feathered trees; 2) proper site preparation; 3) adequate irrigation; 4) tree training; and 5) the correct rootstock/scion combination.

If feathered trees are used, then branches grown in the nursery will develop the spurs for cropping in the second and third leaf.

Proper site preparation includes fumigation, subsoiling, etc., and will provide an opportunity for excellent performance of the new system.

The more dwarfing rootstocks are more sensitive to drought stress. The new planting must have an irrigation system that is flexible enough to irrigate every day or two.

Training is the basic tool used for directing vegetative growth into fruiting wood.

The proper rootstock provides vegetative growth control and induces fruiting. The proper rootstock alone will not guarantee success; it can make the job easier if everything else is done right. The wrong rootstock will aggravate other management errors in pruning, fertilizer, tree training, and tree density.

Garth Kunz Some growers have moved toward high density plantings to add diversity to their apple production and to get into production much more quickly. In British Columbia, some growers have chosen the Dutch slender spindle system for the following reasons:

First of all, it was the system with which they were most familiar, and it gives the earliest production. Because the fruiting wood is being renewed continually, the quality of the fruit remains high during the total productive life of the tree.

Varieties now in production in my orchard on slender spindle are McIntosh, Royal Gala, and Jonagold.

After you understand the slender spindle system, it is a fairly easy system to maintain. It is a system, and the grower must do tree training in a timely manner. The slender spindle system is a disciplined system and requires the grower to be disciplined as well.

Most varieties of apples can be grown on the slender spindle system, except spur types. Delicious, in particular, does not lend itself to the slender spindle. When spur-type Delicious branches are trained down to the horizontal or to a slightly lower position, excessively strong suckers develop on the top of the branches, and the remainder of the branch beyond the suckers becomes too weak to maintain good production.

Four important steps when planning a slender spindle orchard are:

SITE SELECTION AND SOIL PREPARATION

The site should have good air and water drainage. If it is a windy location, windbreaks may be needed. Preparing the new orchard site is very important, especially with inherently weaker size-controlling rootstocks. The soil should be tested at least one year in advance of planting, so any necessary soil treatments can be made. The slender spindle system cannot be planted in an interplant situation. Four reasons for this are:

You cannot correct any soil-related problems.

The young trees will not compete well in the shade of existing trees.

170

Proper training of the new trees is not possible. Proper tree training requires adequate tree growth.

There will be insufficient light for good early fruit bud development. This bud development is a must, if the spindle system is to be successful.

ROOTSTOCK/SUPPORT SYSTEM SELECTION

The first spindle plantings in my orchard were on M 26 rootstocks, spaced 12 feet apart between rows, and trees spaced 6 feet in the rows. The varieties were McIntosh, Gala, and Jonagold. It would have been easier with M 9 rootstocks, as these varieties are very vigorous. Growers should be sure to plant trees with the bud union high enough above the ground to prevent scion rooting. The higher the bud union is above the ground, the more dwarfing effect there is on the tree.

Also, tree quality and training have a tremendous impact. Carefully plan your rootstock selection for soil type, variety, and spacing. The slender spindle system requires support. Here you have a choice, individual stakes of 2 inches minimum diameter by 8 or 10 feet in length, pressure-treated, or a single overhead wire supported by posts and anchors, with smaller diameter stakes for each tree. Be sure your support system will be both strong enough to support tree and crop, as well as lasting for the life of the orchard.

VARIETY AND SPACING SELECTION

Choose the varieties you want to grow and learn all you can about them. You would not want spur-types for the slender spindle system. Plan to maintain the same spacing between rows, however, depending on the variety, the distance in the row can and should be different for different varieties.

TREE QUALITY

To make the slender spindle system really work, you need a tree with a minimum of 8 to 10, 12 to 14 inch feathers (branches). These must be almost horizontal in position at planting time and smaller in diameter than the central leader. Many leading Dutch growers want fruit on the tree in the same year as it is planted. New trees need a second growing season in the nursery, if side branches have not developed. Once you have side branching, care must be taken not to damage them between digging at the nursery and planting in the orchard.

Where insufficient branches developed the year of planting, cut trees back to 32 inches above the ground, and allow only one new leader to develop. This should result in a very good feathered top. It may be too good. If the resulting branches are very strong, they must be trained down in August, or earlier, depending on vigor. Because they are very vigorous, they tend not to develop fruit buds. This puts trees in a very precarious position in the third year, where cropping is required to slow tree growth. By the third year, M 26 roots are quite vigorous, so gaining control of the tree is more difficult. Under these circumstances, the orchard is one full year late on production. When this happens, the economics of the slender spindle system start to fall apart. In the slender spindle, if you try to cut corners on tree quality, you will pay dearly. Tree quality is so important, and yet so many growers have missed it. It is so important, that many leading Dutch growers are now growing their own new trees.

Basic necessity   Tree training is a basic necessity for successfully using the slender spindle system. You should plan to support these trees the year they are planted. It will protect them from movement by wind and greatly assist in tree training. You should not start the branches as low as they do in Holland. For one reason, our weed control is applied during the growing season when low branches hang even lower. When tying trees, never use poly twine, since it will damage trees severely, if not removed in time.

If you have been fortunate and received good, well branched trees, these branches should be tied down to horizontal, or slightly lower, in the first growing season by August, earlier if vigor is high. Remember to keep the crotch angles flat, and avoid an upward arc to reduce sucker growth. These suckers should be removed during the growing season, twice if necessary.

CHOICES IN TRAINING BRANCHES

When training down the branches, we again have a choice. They can be tied down with light string, or, in my opinion, better and faster by using concrete weights approximately 4 ounces in weight. Spreaders do not work as well with the slender spindle system. Another advantage of weights is they can be moved out on the branches as they develop and as the season progresses, or higher in the tree as new branches develop there.

Another option for the grower is to tie the central leader over to horizontal in the first, but also in the second growing season. This can be used to good advantage on very vigorous trees. It will be tied back up the following year after growth starts. If the trees grow well and are trained as described, training the following year will be much easier.

In the following years, the bottom fruiting branches are maintained and retained, but not allowed to become dominant. In the rest of the tree, the fruiting branches are renewed as needed. The top of the tree is kept narrow and not allowed to overgrow the lower portion of the tree. If the top does become too strong, one way to regain control is to remove it and tie up a fruiting branch. This method also helps to reduce the sucker growth which normally develops from this cut.

In conclusion

Summarizing key comments of these three growers should give future high density growers a good structure to build from. First of all, pick a good site. In a high density planting, where trees are close to the ground, frost problems could be unacceptable. Second, plan well ahead to insure you get the rootstock/scion combination you want, and don't accept a compromise. This will mean working much closer with your nursery. Third, use only quality trees that are preferably feathered. This will get your orchard into production earlier, which is a key objective of high density planting. Fourth, make sure that your tree support system is well designed, especially in the area of anchorage. Trellis breakdown after the fifth year will be very costly. Fifth, take the necessary replant steps to assure good young tree growth. Finally, once you've decided on a system, where at all possible, train the trees rather than prune, and do it in a timely manner.

GLOSSARY

Acropetally: movement upward or toward the top (opposite of basipetally).

Apical dominance: the tendency of the terminal bud, or the resulting actively growing shoot tip, to suppress the growth of lateral, lower buds on the shoot.

Auxin(s): hormones which promote cell enlargement and apical dominance.

Bench cut: a heading cut to an outwardly growing lateral, usually of equal or less diameter than the branch being removed and often at an abrupt outward growing angle from the branch portion removed.

Bending: the repositioning of shoots or branches on a tree (*see* limb positioning).

Carbohydrates: a large group of organic compounds composed of carbon, hydrogen, and oxygen. Compounds composed of sugars and starches, which are the products of photosynthesis.

Central leader: 1) A pyramidal-shaped tree with a single vertical stem for the trunk and permanent scaffold branches arising from the trunk from which fruiting wood is renewed. Scaffold branches are usually arranged in tiers with 4 to 5 branches in the lowest tier and usually a smaller number of branches in 1 or 2 upper tiers. Also designed for medium density orchards (PNW central leader, Heinicke central leader). 2) The main vertical central trunk of a tree from which scaffold branches and/or fruiting branches originate.

Competing lateral: a lateral branch or shoot that, because of vigor and/or position, is competing with the main branch on which it is attached.

Cytokinins: hormones associated with cell division and flower initiation.

Desert growing conditions: a climate with characteristics such as high light intensities and low rainfall. In areas such as north central Washington, most of the precipitation occurs as snow; this area is classified as an upland desert because of the relatively high elevation and deep winter.

Dwarf rootstock: any one of a number of specific rootstocks used to restrict the growth of the scion variety. Usually only considered as those rootstocks which reduce scion variety growth by 50 percent or more of a full-sized tree.

Early production: production of fruit early in the life of an orchard, tree, or other producing unit.

EMLA: a series of rootstocks developed by East Malling, Long Ashton Station (EMLA), similar to the original East Malling (EM) series except all latent viruses have been removed by heat treatment. In general, these rootstocks are slightly more vigorous than the corresponding EM series.

Ethylene: a naturally-occurring gaseous hormone that has an inhibitory effect upon growth. It inhibits cell elongation and promotes fruit ripening.

Feathered tree: a branched nursery tree. Also called a "maiden" tree.

Flower buds: buds that produce only flowers *(see* simple buds).

Freestanding tree: a tree (scion) that is grown on a rootstock that does not use mechanical support for anchorage.

Fruit quality: the parameters that define the desirability of fruit, including size, color, and freedom from defects.

Fruit set: the amount of fruit contained by the tree after the period of natural fruit drop in early summer.

Fruit soluble solids: soluble sugars contained within the fruit.

Fruiting habit: the normal pattern of growth within a cultivar leading to the development of fruit buds, flowers, and fruit. In apple, the pattern is typically shoot growth in one season, side shoot and spur development from lateral buds in the second season, and fruit development in the terminal bud position on spurs in the third season.

Growth habit: the type of growth within a cultivar or strain, characterized by vigor, tendency to grow either fruiting spurs or vegetative shoots, narrow or wide branch angles, and upright or more spreading growth. In apples, the growth habit is often characterized by such terms as spur-type or non-spur.

Heading cut (heading back cut): a pruning cut that removes only part of a branch; maybe into 1-year-old wood or older wood.

High density orchard: Orchards planted at more than 500 trees per acre. For example: $6' \times 14'$ (519 trees/acre), $5' \times 12'$ (726 trees/acre), or $4' \times 10'$ (1089 trees/acre) are considered to be high density. Orchards planted at $9' \times 18'$ (269 trees/acre) or $8' \times 18'$ (340 trees/acre) are not considered to be high density.

Horizontal branch angle: a branch spread to a horizontal angle.

Hormone: an organic chemical compound that affects growth when present in very low concentrations.

Interplant: A new tree placed between older permanent trees in an orchard. Interplants may be pollenizers for the main variety. In interplant orchard renewal, older trees are pruned back and eventually removed in favor of the interplanted tree.

Interstem: *see* interstock.

Interstock: a stem piece inserted between the rootstock and scion variety. This piece is often called an intermediate stem piece or interstem. Such a tree is composed of three separate parts – a rootstock, a stem piece, and the scion variety. It is said to have been double-worked.

Labor efficiency: producing the desired result with a minimum of effort, expense, or waste.

Lateral branch: branch or shoot arising from a lateral bud.

Lateral bud: a bud on a shoot arising from the side rather than from the terminal or end position (tip).

Leader bending: bending to a position away from vertical of the central leader of a (spindle) tree to reduce growth of the leader. (The leader may be left permanently bent over with a new leader to assume dominance or later tied upward to resume growth.)

Leader tying: fastening the central leader either downward or upward to the support post or some other structure.

Leaf bud: buds that produce only leaves.

Leaf efficiency: *see* specific leaf weight.

Light distribution: the quantity and quality of light that is received in various locations of the tree's canopy.

Light interception: the total amount of sunlight intercepted by the tree canopy; that light which does not strike the orchard floor.

Limb positioning: the moving or bending of a shoot or branch on a tree to something other than its natural position.

Limb shortening: removal of the main terminal portion of a fruiting branch to a horizontal lateral or downward pointing shoot or spur.

Maintenance pruning: pruning of a mature tree, including pruning for tree size control and renewal pruning.

Meristem: a region in which cell division continues; usually found at apical portions of shoots and roots.

Mixed bud: buds that produce both flowers and leaves.

Non-spur: apple strains or cultivars with a more vigorous growth habit than spur-types, characterized by a greater tendency to initiate and grow longer side shoots on 1-year-old wood rather than spurs.

Non-spur variety: a scion that bears the majority of its crop on weak lateral branches.

Orchard system: an integration of all the horticultural factors involved in establishing and maintaining a planting of fruit trees, including tree density and arrangement, cultivar, rootstock and interstock, tree size and form, pruning and training techniques, and support system, if any.

Permanent branches/tier: branches or branches within a whorl (tier) that are kept for the life of the planting; are not removed in the pruning process.

Photosynthesis: a process in green plants (including apple trees) where carbon dioxide and water are converted, using the energy of the sun, into carbohydrates.

Pinching: the removal of young shoots early in the growing season, commonly done with the fingers.

Precocious rootstock: a rootstock which has the tendency to cause the scion variety grafted onto it to begin bearing earlier in the life of the tree.

Pruning: the judicious removal of plant parts.

Renewal pruning: a type of pruning that continues to encourage the development of the highest quality fruiting wood.

Renovative pruning: corrective pruning, often involving the removal of larger branches in the upper portion of a tree's canopy, to improve the uniformity of light distribution, spur vigor, and fruit quality.

Rootstock: the below ground portion of the tree, either grown from seed (seedling rootstock) or asexually propagated (clonal rootstock) on which the main scion cultivar is budded or grafted.

Runting out: weak growth which results under low vigor conditions, such as overcropping or planting a spur variety on a dwarfing rootstock.

Scion: the upper portion of a fruit tree which is grafted or budded onto the rootstock.

Scion rooting: rooting that occurs from the scion portion of the tree. This often occurs when the scion piece is in direct contact with the soil.

Shading: conditions or tree growth which prevents light penetration and utilization.

Shank: the main rootstock piece extending downward from the bud or graft union to the tip of the rootstock.

Simple bud: a bud that produces either leaves or flowers, not both.

Slender spindle: a small, slender tree form suitable for narrow planting distances in which the framework branches are deliberately kept small and few in number in order to produce a slender cone-shaped tree, generally no bigger than 7 to 8 feet in height and almost always on M 9 rootstocks.

Soil line: the junction of the trunk and root shank at the surface of the soil.

Specific leaf weight: leaf dry weight (DW mg) per unit leaf area (cm²) as an indicator of photosynthetic rate. Synonymous with leaf efficiency.

Spreaders: braces, often stakes of wood with sharp points at either end, used to reposition branches or shoots.

Spreading: the positioning of branches, often to an outward direction or more horizontal angle, with the use of a brace between the main tree trunk and spread branch or the use of twine tied to the ground or a lower branch or support system. Usually done to reduce apical dominance and improve light distribution.

Spur: a shoot whose growth is restricted. Characterized by greatly shortened internodes; appear laterally on branches. In apple (and pear), flowering is largely confined to spurs.

Spur-bound: a weak-growing tree that annually produces little or no extension growth but, instead, directs metabolic resources into an abundance of spurs.

Spur efficiency: total leaf dry weight (DW)/spur as an indicator of spur photosynthetic capacity.

Spur pruning: Pruning which removes spurs or parts of branched spurs, to eliminate weak spurs and reduce fruiting capacity, or improve fruit size and quality.

Spur-type: a genetically-controlled growth habit characterized by apple strains that tend to branch only slightly and, instead of forming side shoots, initiate flowers on terminals of short spurs. Another characteristic, especially in spur Delicious, is to produce very upright growing branches, and dominance of the central leader is not particularly strong. Majority of spurs are located on 2-year-old and older wood.

Spur variety: a scion that bears the majority of its crop on short shoots called spurs.

Staking: supporting a tree with a short or long post or pole to which the tree is attached.

Standard growth habit (also non-spurs): a growth habit showing a greater dominance of the central leader and more inherent vigor than spur-types. Fruit is generally borne on spurs, but also on longer 1-year-old shoots. Generally considered as those cultivars intermediate between "spur-types" and "tip bearers" in the tendency to flower on spurs and larger 1-year-old shoots.

Stubbing: a severe heading cut where only a small portion of the branch remains, often only 1 inch. A renewal pruning cut used to regenerate a fruiting branch. The branch is generally removed to a short (1") stub, and a new shoot from an adventitious bud is allowed to regrow.

Sucker: a shoot, usually vigorous and sappy, growing from an adventitious or dormant bud on the rootstock.

Support system: any of a combination of posts or stakes, possibly in conjunction with wire tied to anchoring weights or devices, used to support and train trees.

Thinning out cut: a pruning cut that removes a branch completely at its origin.

Tip bearer: cultivars that typically bear fruit on the ends of longer 1-year-old shoots instead of spurs. The majority of spurs are located on young 1- and 2-year-old wood. The Rome Beauty growth habit falls in this category.

Transpiration: the loss of water from plant tissues in the form of water vapor.

Tree canopy: the space (3-dimensional) occupied by the branches of a tree.

Tree density: the number of trees per unit area (i.e., acre or hectare) based on in-row and between-row tree spacing.

Tree support: the support system which holds the tree in an aerial position. In the case of freestanding trees, the trunk provides the vertical support and limbs provide crop bearing support. Mechanical support, including a post or trellis system, may be used by the orchardist. Often consists of either stakes or poles by individual trees or posts and wires arranged lengthwise down tree rows with appropriate fasteners to support the tree to the wire.

Tree training: physical techniques that direct the shape, size, and direction of plant growth. The orientation of a plant in space often is the repositioning of shoots on branches on a tree. Often the branches are repositioned with the aid of weights hung from the branches, string or twine tied to the branches being trained, or wooden or metal spreaders placed between the shoot being spread and the central leader. Branches or shoots may be trained in any direction.

Tree vigor: the potential and/or demonstrated amount of tree growth. Rootstock, scion, and horticultural management affect vigor.

Trellis: a support system constructed of posts and wires.

Vegetative bud: buds that do not produce flowers. Also known as "leaf bud."

Vegetative spur: a spur containing no flowers, only leaves.

Vertical axis: a tree form consisting of a single vertical stem for the trunk (vertical axis) which serves to support fruiting branches. The fruiting branches develop around the trunk and are periodically renewed after bending under the weight of the fruit and hence do not become scaffold branches. Fruiting controls vegetative development.

Vertical branch angle: a very upright branch growing in the vertical position.

Water sprout: a shoot, usually vigorous and sappy, growing from an adventitious or dormant bud on the trunk or older branches of the tree.

Whip: an unbranched nursery tree.

Xylem: the principal water-conducting tissue in both herbaceous and woody plants. In apples (and other perennial woody plants), secondary xylem is also formed from familiar annual rings. The spring wood consists of larger cells with thinner walls and appears lighter, or less dense, than summer wood.

Zigzag leader: the characteristic shape of a slender spindle leader, which develops after several years of pruning to replacement laterals.

BOOK DESIGN: *Nancy Born, Yakima, Washington*

COMPOSITION & PRODUCTION: *Donna Walker,* Good Fruit Grower

TYPE: *California, Helios Extended*

PRINTING: *Valley Herald, Spokane, Washington*

BINDING: *Lincoln & Allen, Portland, Oregon*

TEXT PAPER: *Hammermill Offset Opaque Cream White 70 lb., Lustre Finish*

END PAPER: *Speckletone* Cream 70 lb. Text*

COVER PAPER: *Speckletone* Kraft 80 lb. Cover, Antique Finish*
*Speckletone is a recycled paper.

Additional copies of INTENSIVE ORCHARDING:
MANAGING YOUR HIGH PRODUCTION APPLE PLANTING
may be obtained from Good Fruit Grower,
1005 Tieton Drive, Yakima, Washington 98902;
telephone 509/575-2315; Fax 509/453-4880.
The price per copy is $10.00 in U.S. funds,
plus a shipping and handling fee ($3.00 inside U.S.,
$4.00 outside U.S.), if ordered by mail.